JOHNNY CARSON
A Biography

JOHNNY CARSON
A Biography

by Douglas Lorence

DRAKE PUBLISHERS INC.
NEW YORK • LONDON

Published in 1975 by
Drake Publishers Inc.
381 Park Ave. South
New York, N.Y. 10016

Library of Congress Cataloging in Publication Data

Lorence, Douglas.
    Johnny Carson.

    1. Carson, Johnny, 1925—
PN1992.4.C2816   791.45'092'4 [B]   74-22593
ISBN 0-87749-815-6

Printed in the United States of America
0123456789

CONTENTS

Chapter One 1

Chapter Two 19

Chapter Three 31

Chapter Four 59

Chapter Five 69

Chapter Six 101

Chapter Seven 128

Chapter Eight 144

Chapter Nine 164

Chapter Ten 174

Chapter One

He has said it himself many times. It's smart public humility and in all probability it's the truth: "I'm replaceable. Two months after I'm out of here, they'll be saying, Johnny who?"

We all still remember Jack Paar, although many of us now question exactly what it was that we saw in him. Will the man who eventually replaces Johnny be as dissimilar as Johnny was from Paar? Or will NBC, panicky for their night-time millions, race to their computers and try an endless string of media marvels on us until another Paar or Allen or Carson tells them, against their almighty corporate will, that, once again they are doing it all wrong.

If there is one thing certain about late night programming, especially talk shows, it is that the faceless men who run the giant corporations which run the networks, have absolutely no idea of what will work. They've tried practically every-thing—as if somewhere there is a television Koran with the gospel according to Sarnoff, which says that out of ten, fifty, or one hundred shows, one will work.

And so they keep coming, the Cavetts, Douglas's, Griffins, and the Joeys. But they don't work. It seems as if by magic that every weekday night between eight and twelve million people tune in the "Tonight Show," starring Johnny Carson. From 11:00 to 11:30 P.M. the viewer is informed about political assassinations, murders, potential strikes, fires, all the losing home team scores, and a rainy forecast. By then he needs Johnny. And John isn't about to let all those weary millions down. He's out there with the quick patter, the boy-

ish midwestern good looks, and the innocence—double en-
tendres, and ad-libs drift into our bedrooms up between our
spread toes to amuse and tickle us into sleep.

"How about that assassination, huh?"
"What?"
"Last night on the news."
"Oh yeah! But those people are always shooting each
other."
"Did you see Johnathan Winters with Johnny?"
"Thought I'd wet the bed when he said he threw her
out the window."

And so it goes. John often is the subject of many a conversation on the commuter special and on the housewives' hot-
line. If the show was especially good the night before, this is
even more true. The statistics say that one out of every twenty people in the United States watches the show every night.
Yet the first thirty people you talk to have something to say
about the show.

"Shelly Winters is obnoxious."
"She gave Susskind half what he should have gotten!"

The little bits of conversation about the average show vary
depending on how good the show was the night before.
Shows during which Truman Capote calls Jacqueline Susann
a "truck driver in drag," Ed Ames has a hatchet-throwing
exhibition, or Otto Preminger displays his boorishness are
always good for a few perverse laughs.

"Johnny had his number though, right from the very
beginning. . . . The Carnak stuff is awful. How he gets
laughs out of it I'll never know. . . . Funny. The man is
funny."

Sometimes there *is* nothing else to talk about and in true
"Tonight" tradition, it makes little difference whether or not
the event has any meaning outside the show. One night, like

2

it or not, there was Dr. Paul Ehrlich telling us that we had better clean up our acts because the last act was upon us. We had finally lived up to Malthus' dire prediction and had over-populated our planet, practically to the point of no return. We had heard it before: "Prepare! The end is at hand." We were all ready for that. A huge lightning bolt, or maybe a giant fireball with trumpets sounding. But no, nothing quite so theatrical; we were, in a few short years, merely going to fornicate ourselves out of existence.

Ehrlich was sincere and had a sense of humor. But more important, he had all the facts and figures: We are adding seventy million people a year to our planet. The United States has had six hundred thousand battle deaths in all her wars combined; that many people were born on this planet in the last three days.

Johnny was doing his bit. Concerning birth control he had always said, "We're more effective than the Pill."

But Johnny wasn't joking tonight. He was concerned. "Is there something we can do?"

"We must stop having children, before the governments are forced to destroy them!"

Dr. Ehrlich's appearance galvanized America. Z.P.G. (Zero Population Growth) groups found willing ears at last. It was all that was talked about on and off talk shows. The media took up the cry. Politicians began to feel the pressure and introduced legislation designed to force us to live within our means. The mail poured in: "Great! The type of concerned television programming we need more of ... more Dr. Ehrlich!"

Johnny liked Dr. Ehrlich too. We would see more of him. "And if any of you is interested in learning more about the problem, Dr. Ehrlich has written a book entitled *The Population Bomb*, and it will be in bookstores ...," Johnny said on the show one night.

The book sold millions of copies.

A show definitely worth staying up late and tuning in for, but not the biggest "Tonight Show" of all. The granddaddy of them all came about as a falsetto voice uttered the immortal words "I do" to a tennybopper—a media first. The lovely Miss Vicky and Tiny Tim were married on the stage of the "Tonight Show" amid thousands and thousands of flowers. The tulips on stage had been flown in from Holland for the occasion. The groom, dressed in a frock coat, vest, Edwardian top hat, cape and cane, all in silk and satin, had managed to draw the third highest rated audience in the history of television.

The next day few could be found who hadn't been tuned in.

Johnny, Mr. Everyman, had done it again. Everyone thought the show had been done with him in mind.

Some people chattered about the beautiful ceremony, Miss Vicky's Victorian wedding gown, and the flowers. They debated how long it would last. Others remarked about the eccentricity of the couple.

The "hip" crowd knew. Anybody making more than a million a year has to be hip. The rest of the world could buy that Nebraska corn-fed mask Johnny wears, but underneath it, Johnny knew what it was all about—not camp, but CAMP!

But safely tucked away in walnut-paneled conference rooms, high above the millions who tune in every night, sit the men the show was really for. The media hierarchy sat stunned as the show and then the Neilsens hit them right where they understood it—in the pocketbook.

Only the United States government, with billions to spend on rockets and computers, astronauts, and press agencies, had managed to do what Johnny had done with little more than a thousand dollars worth of flowers, some pasteboard for a chapel, a star he had created in the first place, and one teenybopper.

Like him or not, and it would take more than Holmes and Watson on their best day to ferret out a highly-placed executive who did like him, he knew something about television that they didn't—what people, you and me, will turn their televisions on late at night to watch. Then, as now and in the future, it burns them to have one of the hired hands, an entertainer (which makes matters worse) show them how to keep those TV sets all across America burning into the wee hours of the morning.

Despite the attention the Tiny Tim nuptual drew, it was nothing compared to the time Johnny did the one thing no one wanted him to do.

He quit.

During the AFTRA strike of 1967, he rescinded his contract with NBC, claiming they had used taped repeats of previous "Tonight Shows" without his prior consent. By certified letter he informed NBC that he now considered himself a free agent, refusing to become "a scab against myself."

Insiders said NBC could get Johnny to forget his union principles by sweetening his paycheck by one million dollars annually.

Johnny said, "Not so." It was a matter of principle. And so he packed his bags and headed for the sun and sand of Florida, where he said he should be referred to as "an unemployed prince," a reference to a comment he had made on his first evening at the helm of the "Tonight Show."

The press picked up on the misplaced reference to royalty and people began to take sides. NBC planted press release after press release, alluding to how easy it would be to replace him, how much they wanted him back, how they hadn't done anything wrong, how sorry they were even if they had done something wrong. Panic was cheap those two weeks at 30 Rockefeller Plaza.

In the newspapers it was front page news—not an item on the front page—*the* front page . . . "JOHNNY QUITS!"

Airline reservation clerks were deluged as media reporters, columnists, and commentators jumped on the next planes to Ft. Lauderdale to cash in on the biggest story since the impending Arab-Israeli War, which was now cozily situated on page 3 along with everything else going on in the world.

NBC reacted by putting country and western singer Jimmy Dean in John's seat behind the desk just so we would know exactly what we were missing. The ratings plummeted. How could anyone watch? They were all too busy talking about it. With the ratings went the advertisers. Now it was costing money and the panic really set in. Along with it came the newsprint and television news time. CBS and ABC news

5

haven't had a field day like it since.

The ambassador to the United Nations, Adlai E. Stevenson, addressing the American Society of Newspaper Publishers, took note of the fact that the Russians were in the process of colonizing Cuba, and with it the rest of Latin America; Israel and the Arab world were about to enter into a life and death struggle; American soldiers were dying daily in Southeast Asia; there was rioting and strife in our cities and on our campuses. But the big story in the papers was about a talk show host who had quit his job.

Indeed. Not just a talk show host. We still had Joey and Merv and Mike. But *Johnny* had quit. Why all the concern over a man about whom people seemed able to agree on only two points: they liked watching him, and they were at great pains to explain exactly what it was that he did. He didn't sing. The only dancing he did was when "Doc" and the band saw fit to come to his rescue with a soft shoe routine to relieve the tedium of a dying monologue.

He was funny, yes, but not as funny as some. He didn't put them in the aisles the way Rich, or Flip, or Bill, or any one of a number of people he had on his show from time to time did. Johnny is tough to top and he can cut someone to the ground more quickly than anyone, even Rickles. He seldom did that though, preferring to play straight man to others most of the time.

He's not a great interviewer, and seldom does he choose to probe for the hidden insight that will reveal the true character or intentions of his guests.

He's tight about his personal life. Unlike Paar, he never gushed about "Randys" and "Miriams" and other bits of personal family trivia that could give us a vested interest in him.

What does he do then?

Well ... he's entertaining. But is it that simple? Are we that incapable of entertaining ourselves?

"Say listen, most days by 11:30 I'm incapable of undressing myself, let alone entertaining myself."

"Sit back friend. Relax. Johnny knows you don't want to think, and he's not about to force you."

6

Reviewers have called the show "Verbal Muzak" but that's nowhere near the truth. There is no question that the show is as structured as a baseball game. First the monologue, then the comedy bit at the desk, Carnak, Aunt Blabby, or maybe up into the audience for Stump the Band. On to the first guest, budding starlet, tastefully spilling out of her chiffon and tinsel dress. Then to the nightclub singer, and the comic. And bringing up the rear is Dr. Seymour Pothos who has written a book on housebreaking snakes. The book isn't too good, but the doctor has a couple of very funny stories about the time he was held captive for forty-eight hours in the ladies room of a Moscow subway station. That's entertainment?

Not exactly. There is one thing missing. The bartender. The man who will mix all those ingredients and come up with something that will make us laugh and smile more than we have done during the rest of the day. Even if they're all bombs, Johnny, most times, will find something. A leer at the starlet's bosom, the sleepy reaction to a dull story, or a mention of liquor—that's always good for two or three Ed jokes.

> "Ed had his fingers broken last night. The doorman stepped on them as he was coming home."

Johnny knows the territory better than any man alive and seldom will a chance for a laugh get by him. Sometimes, unknowingly, he has trained himself to do exactly this. Since the first time he stepped onto a grade school stage to play Popeye and found that he could make people laugh, he has been an entertainer, most of the time professionally. In fact, with the exception of wartime service, he has done nothing else.

With a sense of timing second to none and a prodigious memory for lines and situations and ways to adapt them to the moment, seldom is he caught with no way to heighten the laughter or to turn a bad situation around.

Change the names, clean it up, and Johnny can use a bit that first worked for him when he was entertaining the men on Guam during the war. Once, while emceeing a beauty contest he quickly memorized all one hundred contestants' names. Ed claims that Johnny can pick up three bridge hands and instantly tell you what's in the fourth. He still does Popeye, as well as anyone. Usually though, Johnny doesn't have to reach that far back. The mix is right. If the singer didn't "wow 'em" the way she did in rehearsals, the comic is attuned to the audience and can do nothing wrong.

And sometimes, not every night or even every week, but sometimes, the mix is just right. It all hits. When that happens, Johnny polishes the chrome a bit, slams a door once or twice, assures us that it has never been driven, and we buy. It's the reason we tune in, it's what we're really waiting for because when the "Tonight Show" really works, it works like little else in the entertainment world. It is light, spontaneous, and as funny as anything you're going to see at any price. Best of all, it isn't something that we laugh at. It's something we laugh with. Johnny has invited us in; he has included us. We know the people and share their enjoyment of the moment, and after the show is over we feel good, we had a good time. It was fun.

Think about it for a minute. How many things could you say that about in the last year; How many TV shows, movies, plays, or books made you feel good last year? That question gives us a clue to how he can drive everything else off the front page. We who buy the newspapers don't know many Arabs or Russians, but we know Johnny. Late at night, he's our friend. We like him, and after a day in the bureaucratic jungle of our world, after we've given *them* another chance to fold, spindle and mutilate us, there he is trying to make us feel good.

The people up in the walnut-paneled rooms never relax long enough to feel good. Why are they so concerned with him? Is he that unique? That irreplaceable? And if they do lose him, what will they be losing?

It's a country that more and more seems to prefer numbers to words . . . "four out of five doctors . . . ninety-nine and forty-four one hundredths percent pure . . . Boston by 3½ over Houston."

And that's where the answer lies. Numbers. None of them small. NBC has a whole department headed by a vice-president whose entire function is to know the numbers. How many are tuned in, where are they, who are they, what do they do for a living, how much of a living do they have to spend on advertised products, who educated them, and who is educating their children?

Paul Klein, vice-president, says that anywhere from two to twelve million people tune in every night, with the average somewhere between nine and ten million. For thirteen years Johnny has been coming into our bedrooms. When all the figures for that time have been added and multiplied, the total comes to a number in the double digit billions.

In the publishing industry it is an accepted fact that an appearance on the "Tonight Show" can be translated into fifty thousand additional books sold. And it doesn't have to be a good appearance. The author can bomb; all that is necessary to reach that fifty thousand figure is for Johnny to hold the book up for the nighttime millions to see. If the author is a hit and the book has something to say, then the numbers are no longer in the tens or hundreds of thousands, but in the millions.

Who do you know who hasn't at one time or another tried one of Dr. Stillman's diets? The very animated and vocal Dr. Stillman is now a regular on the "Tonight Show." He still drops one or two lines about his latest book, but mostly he talks on a variety of subjects. Now he is one of the world's best-selling authors with a string of high-protein diet books. Without knocking the product, it seems highly unlikely that Dr. Irwin Stillman would be a household word without Johnny Carson. The "Tonight Show" has made him a very wealthy man indeed.

The executives in the entertainment industry pay very careful attention to Johnny, too. He has the power to make a "no one" into a "someone." Often a comic or singer who gets one or two good shots on the show finds his telephone ringing nonstop.

The agents are always on the lookout for the latest find from the "Tonight Show."

"I got two weeks in the Lounge at Caesar's Palace for you, sweetheart. Then you go right from there into a split week up at Tahoe . . .."

All of that means numbers. Instead of ninety-five a week from the State of New York, it's thousands from nightclubs and guest shots on other programs.

Many bright, inventive talents have been discovered and promoted by Johnny on the "Tonight Show." Flip Wilson, Bill Cosby, and Rich Little all openly admit that a huge amount of their success has been because of Johnny's ability to reach the numbers he does every night.

Not just unknowns, but stars whose careers are languishing in mediocrity court Johnny because he can change the numbers into millions for the next picture. Burt Reynolds is at times so thankful to Johnny that it gets embarrassing. Johnny always points out, rightfully so, that if performers don't have the talent to come across, there's nothing he can do to make them stars. This is true, but Johnny has the audience and he goes to great lengths to make sure he doesn't lose that audience. An actor can be brilliant on Broadway, but in one night Johnny reaches more people than the Broadway actor could ever reach if he were to play year round without a vacation to packed houses for twelve years.

The right song from a Broadway show sung by the actress on the "Tonight Show" can mean the difference between closing next week and SRO for months to come.

Mediocre or even just plain bad movies are a favorite plug for guests on the show, and it works. Due in large part to the ability to reach the number of people that Johnny does, it is almost impossible to make a picture that loses money so long as the picture budget isn't too big.

Early every fall the parade of has-beens and newcomers with a new series to push is almost endless. John patiently sits and listens to how exciting "XYZ" is, a new series about a hospital anesthesiologist. A short film clip is shown and maybe, just maybe, the series will last for a year or two. The "Tonight Show" can't guarantee success for a new series, but failure to plug the series on the "Tonight Show" is almost certain to result in no one even knowing it was available not to watch.

If there is one group of people in America who understand numbers better than CPA's, it's politicians. Senators who have difficulty getting their wives to listen take an eloquent pose at the prospect of addressing Johnny's millions. Presidential aspirants realize there is no price to be put on a good appearance on the "Tonight Show." Johnny has them all on. The federal government says he has to. The FCC's equal time rule dictates that either all or none must go on. But they never appear together. Everyone gets his or her chance on the soap box, but John isn't about to let them get down into the dirt where they can roll around and upset his audience. He is very protective of us, making sure that we'll still be out here when the next hack ascends.

Roughly twenty minutes of every show is reserved for formal entertainment (singing, dancing, comedy bits, and seal acts). The rest of the program is devoted to commercials and talk.

Johnny sits there night after night listening to the great, the not so great, and the totally unknown. Everyone has a favorite charity, a pet gripe, or a funny story.

> "By the way, John, I'll be opening at Mr. Kelly's on the fourteenth of this month and then . . .."

Doctors plugging for research grants, athletes looking for broadcasting jobs, stars looking for one more shot at the big time, they all come to Johnny and he manages to mix and blend their plugola, funny stories, songs, and gossip with his razor timing and quick ad-libs. He does it so well that seldom are we aware that we have just watched a ninety-minute commercial.

The best part about selling yourself on the "Tonight Show" is that they pay you to do it. It's not a great amount —union minimum, $320. But still, it doesn't cost the guest anything for a shot at the pot of gold and this isn't the case with everyone. Budweiser beer, Sunsweet prune juice, and the thousands of other commercial products hustled to the

American public during the Carson show on NBC don't get paid for the privilege. They pay plenty. It costs close to $20,000 for a minute of Johnny's time. On a yearly basis, those numbers boil down to $30 million in NBC's bank account.

NBS only sells nine network commercials during the show. The rest of the commercials are plugged in during station breaks by the local stations. For the right to do this, they split what they take in with NBC. This is why the number of people tuned in is so important. If the locals feel they can do half as well with a rerun of an old movie they have in their vaults, they can choose not to run the network "Tonight Show" and keep all the profits from the commercials shown during their movie. The chance they take is that some other competing station will pick up the "Tonight Show" and leave them tuned in with six Charlie Chan buffs and no one else to whom to sell their commercial time at any price.

The people with names on their doors at NBC love the numbers generated by Johnny—$30 million a year is certainly music to one's ears. However, it's not nearly as sweet as another figure; what it costs to produce the "Tonight Show."

Raritan Enterprises, Johnny and Sonny Werblin's (ex-financial wizard of MCA, the now defunct giant talent agency) company, produces and sells the "Tonight Show" to NBC for $150,000 a week. Even if the most outlandish rumors of Johnny's salary are used as a basis for computation, this still leaves over $17 million for profit. And, there's no chance involved. It's as guaranteed as the smog in Los Angeles, where the show moved in 1972. Year in, year out, John has pushed the numbers ever higher, and for NBC it keeps getting better and better. The other major networks and every independent network have thrown every imaginable type of competition at him. First run movies, drama specials, rock festivals, confrontation talk shows, sugar and spice talk shows, intellectual talk shows, carbon copy talk shows, and Joey Bishop at least half a dozen times. It doesn't matter. Johnny outdoes them all.

A guaranteed annual income. They must love him in the higher echelons of NBC. The official corporate line is one of

subdued public affection, which uses lots of ambiguous, eso-
teric words. NBC will continue to live with him though; as
long as those numbers are there, they'll live with him. Or will
they? The bigger the stakes get, the easier the egos bruise. All
is peaceful now in Tonightland, but it could erupt again on a
moment's notice, as it has so many times in the past. The
territories are plainly marked; the boundaries are there for
those who want to see them. All it takes is a step into someone else's domain. Standards and practices (the NBC censor-
ing department) could start chopping up Johnny's cute sex
references again. The producer, Fred DeCordova, might begin
to see things differently from John (that's what happened to
the previous producer, Art Stark, who probably still sees
things differently from Johnny—he just isn't the producer any
more). Or John could start to elbow in on some of NBC's
domain. He's done it before and has taken lots of territory.

Everybody gets something out of the "Tonight Show."
The audience gets entertained; the guests get to sell their
movies, plays, books, specials, etc.; Budweiser gets to sell
beer; NBC gets to sell it's time; and Johnny . . . what does
Johnny get out of all this?

Lots! Not as much as many entertainers and definitely not
as much as some others might demand in his position, but
certainly something. It is big time entertainment, long past
the days of the nickelodeon. But if Johnny were to get just
five cents every time someone tuned into the "Tonight
Show," his salary would amount to over $100 million a year.
NBC does not pay him that much. What NBC does pay him,
exactly, is a closely guarded secret, known only to NBC,
Johnny, and the lawyers involved. The exact amount will
never be known because one of the clauses in the contract
specifies that neither NBC nor Johnny will ever disclose any
of the other clauses. To arrive at a number, then, we are left
with rumors and educated guesses. At the time of his return
after the 1967 walkout, the *New York Times* ran a story
reporting that Johnny's settlement with NBC called for a
weekly salary of $75,000.

Not so, claimed Johnny, and "informed sources" put his
weekly paycheck at a much more realistic $55,000. Eight

years later the $55,000 figure is still the number handed out by NBC if someone presses them hard enough. This does not take into consideration the reported RCA stock, million-dollar life insurance policy, and other bonuses NBC sends Johnny's way to keep him happy. He also gets an official thirteen weeks off a year with some form of compensation. Part of his vacation time he spends in Las Vegas with his night club act, for which he is reportedly paid in excess of $40,000 a week. Sonny Werblin and Johnny are the sole owners of Raritan Enterprises, and it can be safely assumed that part of the $150,000 a week NBC pays to Raritan for producing the "Tonight Show" must in some way go to John. NBC also employs Raritan to "develop" new show ideas. The "Sun City Scandals" and other TV specials came out of this. He and Sonny are also involved in Johnny Carson Clothes, which dumps more wampum into the Carson pocket. Despite the occasional wincing and moaning over the amount he has to pay in alimony, there appears to be plenty for John to spend on his myriad "interests." Johnny doesn't like the word hobbies, so he doesn't have any "hobbies," only "interests." Some of Johnny's interests have been water skiing, bowling, flying, guitar, drums, home videotape, astronomy, tennis, scuba diving, and boating. He sees something that intrigues him and throws himself into it completely until he reaches a certain level of competence. Then he puts it down just as abruptly as he picked it up, not to be picked up again. His tolerance for boredom is certainly not high. The many interests are also a form of work. It helps if he knows first hand what his guests are talking about.

Johnny also gets something else from the "Tonight Show." When John wears turtleneck sweaters, a lot of other people do, too. He started a rush for Nehru jackets in the middle sixties. He once repeated an obscure comment, by an even more obscure congressman, concerning a possible shortage of toilet tissue and started a stampede of panicky housewives across America to stockpile toilet paper. Many stores were forced to put a limit of several to a customer to keep from running out. He is the only man in the world who can literally "make a star overnight." There is no one in America, save those with personal grudges, who would not pick up the telephone were he told Johnny was on the other end.

This is a long way from doing a magic act for twelve people at a Christmas party at the Wahoo Hatchery in Wahoo, Nebraska to his first real broadcasting job for $47.50 a week at Station WOW, Omaha, Nebraska, to millions of dollars and superstardom on the "Tonight Show."

Outwardly, at least, from what we see on television, Johnny hasn't changed. When we settle back to watch the show, he pops through the curtains with his graying, boyish good looks, that midwestern folksy attitude, and we can put our feet up to relax with someone we've known a long time. He's our friend.

In the early sixties, one of the first extras he demanded— and got—from NBC was a chauffeur-driven limousine to whisk him daily between his apartment and the studio. This was effected to eliminate any chance, no matter how inadvertent, that he might come in contact with the public. On several occasions John has confessed to a recurring nightmare in which he is caught at curbside without a taxi in sight as the cry goes up from a herd of housewives. Without doubt, a thought to strike terror in the stoutest of hearts, but John goes to even more elaborate lengths to insure that neither his body nor his mind will be bothered by this encounter.

Some of his fears concerning contact with his public are rooted in past experience. He has had arms grab and pull him into alleys to hear child prodigies sing; total strangers sit down to join him for dinner; he met his second wife through her father, who was trying to audition another violin-playing daughter.

John recounts the stories, but they aren't the reason he gives for staying locked up tight, away from the public, the press, and for the most part, away from the rest of the show business crowd.

"I think I owe one thing to my public—the best performance I can give. What else do they want from me?" he adds.

Probably the same thing they'd want from anyone else they let into their bedrooms. After five nights a week for thirteen years, we know Johnny pretty well. Is he a

Republican or a Democrat? What does he think about busing? There must be some entertainment personalities he simply can't stand. Whom does he watch on television? What does he like to eat? What kind of car does he drive? Are his kids "hippies"?

As his second banana for eighteen years, Ed McMahon says, "Johnny packs a tight suitcase." And with a lock on it, and John is the only one with a key. Interviewer after interviewer has come up with little more than could be learned by watching the show. Whenever John is asked about his early life, his face becomes pained as he replies, "Do we have to talk about that?"

A good deal of the ambiguities come from John's tenacious guarding of the numbers. Don't say anything about Republicans, or the Democrats might not tune in. The wrong references to busing, and he could lose an entire state. As long as he can keep those Neilsen numbers up, he has an iron-clad guarantee that his one-sided love affair can continue.

But don't think for a minute that the adulation isn't important to him. It is, and he works as hard if not harder than any man in television to see that he'll always have an audience to hide from.

The time he spends with us every night, seven and a half hours a week, would be a good chunk of anyone's life. To Johnny, it's practically his entire life; practically everything in his life relates in some way to those seven and a half on-camera hours. To put into perspective exactly what seven and a half hours of programming means in the way of work, think for a minute that most hour and a half motion pictures take the better part of three months, from beginning of shooting to completed product. This does not take into consideration the time needed to write the script; nor does it reflect the weeks and months of preproduction planning, costing, location scouting, casting, and the myriad of other elements involved in a theatrical production.

A one-hour TV special could take up to four weeks to complete. One sequence of a television series, with its rigid format and unvarying plot and characters, often takes a whole week to tape, and nine times out of ten is nowhere nearly as entertaining as the "Tonight Show."

In one week it is as if Johnny and his "Tonight" staff put together and get on the air two full-length movies, three TV specials, and three editions of the evening news. Not only that, with so many other jobs, there's no way he can merely show up. He has to be there and be *on*. He is on camera 80 percent of those seven and a half hours. In anybody's language, that's a grind, and it can be terribly debilitating, exhausting a person in a matter of days, as it so often does with his substitute hosts.

Aware of the effects of fatigue, John takes more time off than anyone else scheduled for the entire fifty-two weeks a year. It isn't so much the personal affects of the strain that seem to bother John as it is the loss of the kind of performance he feels he should give to the show every night. Not a man to cry in public or even make legitimate excuses, he merely takes the time off and lets the public think what they will. As with everything he does, if Johnny is convinced it is right, he does it, never feeling the need to justify his actions. This may lead to many misunderstandings and ill feelings. Many say if he would just explain himself once in a while, some of these problems would never come up. But as Johnny says, "I think I owe one thing to my public—the best performance I can give."

And it ends right there. For to explain might give someone ammunition to use against him, and that is not good. Johnny feels people have used him on more than one occasion. This is understandable. There is no one who has something to sell—whether it be himself, his ideas, books, or prune juice—who can't benefit from an association with Johnny.

Many people have benefited, some more than Johnny himself. Until a few years ago when Sonny Werblin took over as his financial counselor, it was rumored that Ed McMahon could buy and sell John. That isn't the case today.

The problem, however, does exist, and it is uniquely Johnny's own because no one else is capable of benefiting so many people from nothing more than an association. How can he be sure of anyone? He can't. And unlike most visibly successful personalities who have become reconciled to a certain amount of abuse, he locks himself up, away from those who might want something. He doesn't feel that he owes anyone anything. There are no mysteries as to how he got where he is, and Johnny feels no pressure of implied obligations to spread it around. Since his earliest days as a boy magician back in Nebraska, on through all his broadcasting and telecasting contacts, one thing that was never found lacking in John was ambition; and it was ambition, coupled with a lot of hard work, that got him where he is today.

Almost at the pinnacle, it is hard to imagine John with more power or influence. He can still grab for more money, but says, "It's silly to have as one's sole object in life, just making money, accumulating wealth. I work because I *enjoy* what I'm doing, and the fact that I make money at it—big money—is a fine-and-dandy side fact. Money gives me just one big thing that's really important—the freedom of not having to worry about money. It gives me the freedom to worry about the things that really matter."

He has arrived at a position of power and wealth envied by millions and says of it, "I wouldn't call myself a great deal happier now than when I was earning $47.50 a week in Omaha."

Chapter Two

It is the state of Nebraska that generally (and proudly) takes the credit for being Johnny's birthplace and home, and, indeed, it is Nebraska that Johnny acknowledges as such. But actually Johnny was born in Corning, Iowa on October 23, 1925. He spent his early childhood in the small towns of southwestern Iowa, tiny little pimples of houses, silos and barns clumped together in that vast never-ending expanse of fertile land known as America's grain basket.

What was exciting in Clarinda and Shenandoah was whose father had just purchased a new tractor and the latest reaper from International Harvester. Television and radio hadn't linked these places to the rest of the world yet. There were still real "country folk" to be found, and you could become "someone" by impressing only a couple of people. An easier time; it wasn't a bad life.

Johnny was the middle child of Homer and Ruth Hook Carson. He has an older sister, Catherine, and a brother Dick who was later to direct the "Tonight Show."

Homer, or "Kit" as he was known, was a lineman for the power district of the Nebraska Power and Light Company. Somewhat self-consciously Johnny identifies him today as "a guy who climbed up and down telephone poles."

The family moved a lot in those early years as the elder Carson's job dictated, and when John came of school age, he found himself in Avoca. There were fewer than 1,500 people living in the entire town of Avoca then. By the time Johnny was eight, his father has been promoted to supervisor and the family moved to eastern Nebraska, where they settled permanently in Norfolk—population 15,000.

While Kit was looking for a house, he temporarily boarded the family in a hotel in the center of town. At eight years old, John was convinced that Norfolk was the biggest city in the world. He had never seen anything like it and still recalls, with a slight touch of awe, "looking down from the fourth floor hotel window there and thinking how high up I was and marveling at so much traffic."

Kit finally found a big frame house in which the children grew up the same as any other middle-class family in town. John has always insisted that there was nothing unusual about his childhood.

He and his brother fished and skinny-dipped in the big windy Elkhorn River before it made its way on to the Platte and out into the Missouri. He had his chores and pets and bicycles, the same as millions of other kids across the country. In the summers the family vacationed in the lake country of Minnesota. Relaxed and easy, that was the way it was—not being expected to generate the drive and ambition necessary to get to the top and stay there for so many years.

Looking back, his brother remembers, "Put it this way; we're not Italians. Nobody in our family ever says what he really thinks or feels to anyone else." But then there are some people who just have to *know*—know how a ball point pen works, how many people live in Tokyo, why it rains. They'll go to elaborate lengths just to know how far they can jump, how good they are, how well liked, how handsome, how smart and how funny. If there's no one telling you, there has to be some other way of finding out.

Appearing in a school play as Popeye, Johnny heard people laugh at hime for the first time. It was here, and he still remembers it vividly, that he found he could make people laugh. It was a revelation, a new avenue of communication. His family as well as other people conveyed their acceptance of him through laughter. So he continued, first with voices, then with whole comedy bits.

John claims never to have thought about becoming an entertainer. He always just says, "People thought I was funny."

Once, while lolling around a friend's house, John happened to pick up a book and started thumbing through it. The book was Hoffman's *Book of Magic*. It described all the standard tricks, instructed how to confound and confuse an audience with them, and how to make the basic equipment. John's interest was aroused. In the back of the book a magic kit was advertised. The copy said the kit would make you the "life of the party," with this kit you would now be able to "mystify and amaze your friends."

Johnny says that he got into magic in order to overcome a basic shyness. It's pretty safe to assume that the young John wasn't the "life of the party," nor was he "amazing" to many of his friends.

He sent to Chicago for the magic kit and from that moment on, he could think of nothing but magic. Locked in his room for hours on end, he practiced endlessly linking rings, multiplying balls, doing the rope cutting trick, changing colored scarves. He was twelve years old and there was nothing else in his life.

He ordered, read, and reread every magic catalogue he could get his hands on. And kept on practicing. His family today recalls that they almost had to move out of the house to keep the pesty little magician out of their hair. Any audience would do. "Here, pick a card," he would say as he practiced on them. He was beginning to master it; just a little more practice.

His mother thought John should get some form of musical training and sent him to learn piano from Cora Beals. The lessons were twenty-five cents an hour. But piano wasn't what interested him. John wasn't headed for concert halls or smoky cellars of jazz bars, at least not as a musician. Magic was all he cared about, and he spent every cent on more equipment, better tricks, anything to improve his act. Very few of the quarters his mother gave him ever found their way to Cora Beals. They were mailed straight to Chicago to be redeemed for more magic, better tricks.

John always loved cards and still pays close attention to those who work with cards on the "Tonight Show." He constantly had a deck in his hands. "Pick a card, pick a card!" became a standard cry around the big frame house. Once totally enthralled by a new trick he had mastered, he frantically raced about the house looking for someone to impress, finally bursting into the bathroom where his mother was seated, saying, you guessed it, "Pick a card."

His sister Catherine today says, "Anytime we want to ride John, all we have to say is, 'pick a card.' "

People began watching John; they paid careful attention to his magic. While his hands were moving with the multiplying balls, he was the center; all things radiated from him as long as he could continue to mystify and amaze. More quarters to Chicago, less to Cora.

One Christmas Ruth Carson gave up on getting her son interested in music. She sewed a black banner with large Chinese letters, "THE GREAT CARSONI." Along with it, she made a matching black cape, all of which accompanied a magic table, purchased from Chicago by Mr. and Mrs. Carson with more than quarters. This was a real magician's table, something that required a real magician.

Johnny remembers it in tones reserved for those once-in-a-lifetime dreams come true: "I have never since seen anything more beautiful than that was to me."

That table was probably used more than any gift any parent has ever given. With it John became more and more polished. The time was rapidly approaching when he would move on from casually entertaining friends and relatives to a real performance in which you enter and exit. There's a big difference between the two. The risk of failure when a deck of cards is casually pulled out is minimal. When you commit yourself to perform, however, that's exactly what you had better do. No mistakes. People have come specifically to watch you. For a premiere John picked the biggest pressure cooker there is for a twelve year old—his mother's bridge club. Every single woman at a bridge club will swear their own son is the most talented in the world. Apparently John pulled it off, probably in the true Carson fashion—prepared, rehearsed, no surprises.

He was into it now, and he moved on from the bridge club to anyone who would have him. Sunday school parties, church picnics, school socials, anywhere there were people. During those years any group of people that could loosely be termed an audience included "THE GREAT CARSONI." And John dazzled them with card fans and rolling quarters over his knuckles. Perform, entertain—that was his credo now.

John always had trouble being with people; he was ill at ease with people in an impromptu situation. But in a situation where he knew what was to happen, where he could control the events, that was different. Then there were no surprises. Things went the way John said they were to go. The only deviation would be if he made a mistake. And there were no mistakes, no surprises. He practiced and practiced to insure that.

He was always perfecting his act. John knew how to keep his audience guessing, just a little bit more. There was never a long wait until the next time. John knew that with each audience, he was polishing his act that much more. A little light comedy between the tricks turned a young boy's routine magic act into something more personal; he was Norfolk's own magician. They all knew the skinny kid with the black cape, the top hat, and that "GREAT CARSONI" magic table.

Still devouring magic catalogues, he was always trying new tricks, a different twist here, a better way there, always polishing, forever looking for the next audience to entertain, and get that applause. The time had arrived for the aspiring Dunninger to make the next giant step. He would now do his act for money, become a professional. With money you don't fool around, especially in conservative post-Depression Nebraska. He had to make sure he was good because he was asking for a bit of the sweat off a farmer's brow in return for a half hour of illusion.

The Norfolk Rotary Club was his first professional appearance. He received $3.00 for the gig. The die was cast.

As a child professional entertainer John Carson was a success. At $3.00 a show he opened new ground—4-H clubs, county fairs. More and better magic came by mail from Chicago. Firemen's picnics, the Chamber of Commerce, and money began to add up. In small-town Nebraska, $3.00 in the 30's was a lot more than it is today. You could buy the best meal in Norfolk for $3.00. You could go out on a lavish fourteen-year-old date for $3.00.

John went steady with a girl for a year in high school but other than that, he won't discuss any other dates. He'll discuss the magic though, which is how most of his time was spent. "Every kid growing up has happy times and unhappy times," he says today of his childhood. The "happy times" for John were obviously spent entertaining. Working hard to prepare his act, then receiving the anticipated appreciation was then as now, what was important to him.

Once again he sent to Chicago, this time for a $15.00 course in ventriloquism. With more practice and more time, it too was soon added to the act. John didn't work with a dummy, he threw his voice and used the effects he could generate in the act. He also had a great deal of fun with his newly learned ability.

Stories crop up and press agents get hold of them. Before long they become fact—such as the alleged time at the county fair that John threw his voice into a cow's mouth.

Johnny says he has no recollection of the event. That seems strange because there are, at the very least, three hundred people in Norfolk who will swear they were "with Johnny at the time." Such is stardom. People like to remember the little human things that the big stars did. There is hardly a person over the age of twenty in Norfolk today who won't swear they had him "picked as a winner" long before the rest of the world ever knew his name.

Most of this is, of course, just talk, but of the people who were in Norfolk when John was growing up, practically all knew him. It was a small town, yes, and Johnny was a local personality. He was a "somebody" then. He performed anywhere, on top of trunks, on two boards laid across a couple of fuel drums. With a smile, John remembers setting up his act inside a huge chicken shed with the chickens still milling and clucking about his feet. The occasion was the Christmas show for the employees of the Wahoo hatchery—all twelve of them. Not everyone starts on Broadway.

At fourteen John was selected along with other young performers to barnstorm the state for the Chamber of Commerce. As the big flatbed truck would roll into a town and the crew would start to unload and set up the show, it was John's job to act as the barker or pitchman, drawing the crowd around for the show. He would do the whole pitchman bit with some magic and a touch of ventriloquism thrown in.

"Step right up, step right up. You people in front want to sit down so those in back can get a look."

There were new and different audiences every day. These had to be happy times.

"Now, you'll notice I have here five solid steel rings. Would you please examine this? Watch carefully . . .."

By the time John entered high school, he was earning good pin money with his act. In school he participated in anything and everything. The first day at football practice the less than mammoth Johnny carried the ball and was tackled hard. The next thing he remembers is the coach's face looking down into his glassy eyes.

"Are you all right?" the coach asked.

Groggily, John stood up and tried to get his bearings.

"There are a lot of other activities someone your size should get involved with," he was told.

And so, wholeheartedly, John threw himself into "other activities." He appeared in every school play. He had written all his own material for his act and now he started writing the comedy column for his school paper. Singlemindedness has always been one of John's stronger traits. In wartime America there were many activities we participated in as a nation. Victory gardens and bond rallies, as well as paper and scrap metal drives were favorites. Johnny was in charge of the scrap metal drive for his high school and he attacked it as he did anything else. He already knew what hard work got you and he expected hard work from everyone.

Working for John then could have been just as difficult as some people find it today. He doesn't tolerate too much wasting time. Sometimes it was easier just to hide. One evening he could find no one to go out on a drive he had organized. Since Johnny was not one to waste too much time looking, he went out by himself. The next morning, in the middle of the school parking lot, where all the scrap collected was to be heaped, there stood a huge hay rake, weighing a thousand pounds, at least. Later that day a less than pleased farmer came and retrieved his property. John was mum. To this day he has never told anyone how that hay rake got into the school parking lot.

He also managed to find willing hands for the next scrap metal outing. It didn't matter though; Johnny was finding out slowly but surely he could do it himself. He didn't need other people. The question was, how far could he go by himself?

His childhood and adolescence were drawing to a close. The strict Protestant confines of middle-class Nebraska were about to turn him loose. He was marked, however, with a strong sense of right and wrong—not just legal right and wrong, but the things puritanical morality dictated as right and wrong, proper and improper, etc. He didn't know it then, but this background would come in very handy later.

Upon graduation from high school one of his teachers scribbled in his yearbook, "You have the ability to make people laugh. You will go far in the entertainment world." Someone in Norfolk had the foresight to write it down, although we know today that many were thinking the same thing.

That summer John was accepted into the Navy's V-12 program as an air cadet. He had the rest of the summer off before the program started in the fall. He took the time to hitchhike to California.

Even then, Norfolk was not like Hollywood. The awestruck John made his way around the city agog. He noticed that servicemen got everything. They got into the canteens free; they got into the best shows free; they got into everything for free. And they got all the women too. This was wartime, and what better way to show our gratitude than to let the GI's have it all for nothing. Enterprising as always, John made his way to the first Army-Navy store he could find and decked himself out in uniform. He headed for the servicemen's shows and intently watched the people who got big money for entertaining.

JOHNNY CARSON

Hearing that Orson Welles, the great director, was doing his magic act for servicemen in San Diego, John headed south. Situating himself as close to the stage as possible, he was ready when Orson asked for an assistant. John scrambled up onto the stage and was happily sawed in half by the great director. It was his first taste of the big time.

Later that night he experienced another first at two MP's approached him, asking for identification and then charging him with impersonating a serviceman. The bail was fifty dollars.

He returned to Nebraska in September only to find that there were no openings in the air cadet program—the sole reason he enlisted. John was to be sent, instead, to Columbia University's midshipmen's school. He had set out to fly, and now they were going to stick him on a barge in the middle of the Pacific. The news didn't sit well with him. In fact, it didn't sit well with him for twenty years. It was that long before John had the opportunity to learn to fly. After he had mastered it, he let it be. John does almost no piloting today. He didn't want to learn how to fly because of an uncontrollable urge to race about the heavens. It was merely something he had started out to do twenty years before and had finally gotten around to finishing. If the government wouldn't help him, then he'd just do it himself.

After graduating midshipmen's school, John spent a year on drab Navy bases in the deep South. Of that year, most of all, he remembers the boredom. Plenty of time on his hands; it was typical stateside military life. But Johnny found a way out of the boredom. He had brought a footlocker of gear along with him. Now he had a new audience. The men he served with were no less bored than he was. An entertainer in their midst was almost as good as finding a girl in their midst.

He loved it. "If you're an entertainer, if you can do anything to make people laugh, you're always in demand in the service. And the audiences are very good and very forgiving. It's a marvelous training ground for a performer because you always have an audience," Johnny remarked.

To someone who had spent the last six years looking for audiences, the service couldn't have been that hard to take.

27

The act was getting more and more comedy. He still relied heavily on the magic, especially if the audience were one he was unfamiliar with. But slowly he was beginning to make the transition from "THE GREAT CARSONI" to Johnny Carson.

"Funny thing, though," Johnny says today, "I still didn't have any intention of entertaining as a serious career. I was still very small town in my outlook. It would be another three years before I'd find out that the Catskills weren't a dance team."

It was still pin money and something he enjoyed doing. Finally assigned to the battleship "Pensylvania" in the Pacific, John packed up the footlocker and shipped out to new audiences. On the "Pennsylvania" he was one of the few officers who entertained the enlisted men. The act took on a decidedly anti-officer tint and the men loved it. He didn't like the vice presidents in the Navy any more than he was later to like them in television.

On a ship in the middle of the ocean there's even less to do than there is in Norfolk. Johnny was in demand and he performed at every opportunity. He perfected and polished the act and used the hours of endless tedium out on the ocean to work up new gimmicks and twists.

When new orders came, John found he was headed for Guam. When inquiring about what the island was like, he was told, "They're going to love you, John. There's less to do there than there is on this ship!"

He decided to add something new as long as he was, once again, going to be stuck with plenty of time. From the mail-order house in Chicago he ordered a ventriloquist's dummy. He'd never worked with one before, but he felt the forgiving military audiences were the best places to break it in.

Arriving in Guam, he found the dire predictions a reality. But there was someone waiting for him when he got there. "Eddie" had arrived in the mail from Chicago. John went straight to work with the new addition to his act.

Today, when talking about Eddie, he will discuss at length the idiosyncrasy that all ventriloquists share. They all, deep down inside, believe that the dummy is alive. Watch Edgar

Bergen. There is no way he could do the act he does without believing in the life of Charlie. John has analyzed in great detail practically all forms of entertaining and is capable of dealing with other ventriloquists' dummys in clinical detail. Watch him sometime when he's talking about his own ventriloquist act. That isn't wood, paint, and cloth he's talking about—it's Eddie.

All through the service John found it handy to keep his tuxedo pressed and ready. He would speak off base after hours and perform for the civilians for some extra money. There was nowhere to sneak to on the "Pensylvania," but now he was back in business again.

One night he was called on to decode an important message that had just come in. He tackled the problem and stayed up all night, finally delivering the message to the admiral over breakfast. With the admiral was Secretary of the Navy James Forrestal.

"What are you going to do after the war, son?" the secretary wanted to know.

Up until this time John hadn't given it much thought, beyond maybe a journalist or an engineer, but he responded with, "I was thinking of becoming an entertainer, sir."

He spent the next several hours entertaining the admiral and Mr. Forrestal with card tricks and a few hearty laughs.

The mighty war machine the U.S. had built was winding down, and some of the living were heading back stateside. John drew the *U.S.S. "Pennsylvania"* again, except this time she had been torpedoed, and was going back for repairs. They patched the hull sufficiently to get her across the Pacific, but not much better. In the stern, where the damage was the worst, they set up pumps that ran continually to keep the seeping water down to an acceptable level. John's job was to watch the pumps. What he was to do if something happened is not clear because he didn't know much about pumps.

Luckily, nothing went wrong, so there was John once more with lots of time on his hands. He used the time in the bowels of that moaning creaking hulk of steel to practice the throwing of his voice at greater distances. The young boyish ensign would quietly sit tending his pumps as sailors ran from companionway to ladder to deck, frantically trying to ferret out the mystery person. Johnny gave them all the help he could, which wasn't much, since he "had those pumps to tend."

Once on the West Coast, his last detail was as officer in charge of a troop train heading East. To this day, Ed McMahon delights in coaxing stories out of Johnny about that train ride. A train load of sailors headed for discharge at the end of a war would be a rough package for a company of MP's to handle. For a twenty-one-year-old ensign who looked as if he could count the times he had shaved on the fingers of one hand, it was an impossibility. Johnny still isn't sure whether or not they all got to their destinations.

After his discharge, John applied under the GI bill to the University of Nebraska, in Lincoln. He had made up his mind. He was going to become a journalist.

Chapter Three

The University of Nebraska at Lincoln is one of those huge state institutions that is easy to get lost in—for most people, that is. Drinking beer, the eternal search for women, and making it to as many classes as the other two activities will allow is the way many men spend their allotted time in college.

This was not the case with overachieving Johnny. He threw himself 100 percent into everything. With his act polished from two years in the military, he hit the service club trail again, doing his magic, comedy, and ventriloquism for Elks, Moose, Rotarians, fraternities, and anyone else who would hire him. Prices had gone up, and now he was beginning to make some decent pin money.

In addition to entertaining his fellow sailors and whatever other duties the Navy had assigned him, John picked up credits in chemistry and calculus and learned to type. He thought typing would help him in his journalism course, which, in turn, he thought would give him a good basis for eventually writing comedy.

Soon, however, the journalism began to wear on him. "That who-what-where-when bit couldn't have bored me more, so I switched to radio and speech."

He joined the Phi Gamma Delta fraternity, but soon realized it was a mistake. For one thing, he was not a kid fresh out of his mother's arms and high school. He had been earning his own money since he was fourteen and had just finished two years of the most serious business there is; he participated in all that goes along with being a "brother."

Always being able to turn the most adverse situation to an

31

advantage is a trait that has produced some of Johnny's funnier moments. He learned it early and was ready when his old car finally gave up and died. He had it towed to the back of the fraternity house where he rented it out as a lover's paradise for twenty-five cents an hour. With gas rationing cutting into everyone's mobility, he soon turned the old hulk into a money-making success.

In his senior year, he starred as Cleopatra in a frat revue entitled "She Was Only a Pharaoh's Daughter, But She Never Became a Mummy," but long before that, he had recognized the obvious: that fraternities were not set up to include students, but to exclude other students.

With a sharp eye to finding his place in the scheme of things, John worked as hard in the frat revue as he had at the magic, ventriloquism, and all the other entertainment endeavors because he was keenly aware of who was included and who was excluded. Never included until he made it into the most exclusive "in" group of them all, that of the Super Stars, he knew there was no way to maintain one's individuality and still be accepted.

"The word that's always applied to me is aloof, or private, or any combination of those two. That's me. I didn't invent it. I was that way in high school, although then the word was 'conceited.' It's easy to be popular, but you also become a carrot in the meantime."

Very few "carrots" reach the plateau of super stardom where the only criterion for continued acceptance is the ability to do the one thing John does more consistently than anyone else: entertain.

Through the radio and speech department, John became fascinated with the still-infant medium of television. Today when critics tear TV apart for its lack of sophistication, comparing it to the other communication mediums, John becomes more than a little annoyed and is quick to point out the relative youth of the industry. "My first TV broadcast was when I was at the University of Nebraska. You know what the broadcast range of that show was? The cameras were in the university theater's basement and the screen was up in the auditorium, and that was the first television at the university. That was 1949; *that's* how young television is."

From the beginnings in the auditorium he soon branched out into "real" broadcasting with his first professional job at station KFAB in Lincoln, playing in a Western comedy, "Eddie Sosby and the Radio Rangers." The show was broadcast three mornings a week and John had to get permission on those days to be fifteen minutes late for his Spanish classes.

By now John had made up his mind that his future was in broadcasting. No stranger to hard work and study he began an analysis of broadcast comedy that he is still in the midst of today. He became obsessed with the great radio comedians and their routines, choosing comedy as the subject for his senior thesis. In typical Carson fashion it was thorough, detailed, and just a little bit different. Instead of merely writing about timing, building punch lines, sequence, and running gags, John taped segments of the programs to illustrate his points. Using the best of Fibber MacGee and Molly, Jack Benny, Milton Berle, and Bob Hope, he pointed out the extremely delicate nature of comedy, the need for the proper build up, and the great importance of timing.

After listening to it recently he said, "It was a bit naive, but not bad for 18 years ago."

Before handing in the thesis, a friend took Johnny to Omaha to meet his father, Bill Weisman, who was the assistant general manager of radio station WOW. Weisman got John an interview and audition, which must have gone pretty well. When John took the cap and gown off after graduation, he went directly to Omaha and his new home at WOW. His salary was $47.50 a week.

John started as low man on the totem pole at WOW, and for that $47.50, he was required to do everything and anything: commercials, station breaks, weather reports, sweeping out the studio, and locking up at night. He loved it. Each day presented something new, and each day Johnny brought something new to the job. Even people who had seldom listened to the radio knew of him as he carved out a niche as

Omaha's resident "crazy."

One of his best remembered stunts from those radio days came about as the city tried to get rid of the pigeons then defacing the Omaha city hall, a problem most big cities with huge old Victorian municipal buildings must face sooner or later. Omaha, as so many other cities, decided the most efficient and humane way to dispose of the problem would be with poison. What made Omaha's problem unique was the young radio personality at WOW who took up the side of the pigeons in the dispute.

It was not long before Johnny had rallied support for the doomed birds, and as the storm over the birds ebbed and flowed he kept adding more fuel with bright little bits like interviews with condemned pigeons.

He would ask the birds for their side of the controversy and then, after several pathetic "coos" were heard, he would act as an interpreter. "Please, we're nothing but defenseless creatures. Why do you want to kill us?"

Day after day the city postponed placing the poison out for the pigeons until finally a natural gas company, sensing the free publicity, came on the air donating the ledges and window sills of their office building for the birds to habituate.

Although $47.50 is not a lot of money, you could have lived on it in the 1950's in Omaha. John and some of the other guys then working for WOW used to sit around after work talking and dreaming of the day when they would be earning $150. Even the overambitious Johnny would have found it hard to conceive of the money he now earns.

Then, he had to be satisfied with the salary at WOW and what he could pick up on the side with his magic and ventriloquism. He was getting $25.00 and more for afterwork gigs.

Another decision that was to have a great effect on his life was hiring a pretty young coed named Jody Wolcot as his new assistant in the magic act he had been regularly earning his living with. This was before his days at WOW, but Jody stayed with him, later to become his wife. His first son was born within a year after their marriage.

At the station John was taking on more responsibility.

Television, still in its infancy, was making its first appearance in Omaha, and now John, in addition to his morning radio program and other duties, took on an afternoon television slot.

Those were the days of ten-inch screens housed in four foot by four foot cabinets, fuzzy pictures that lapsed into snow on a moment's notice, test patterns, and "Howdy Doody." Everyone knew as much about the new medium as the next man, so someone with as many new ideas as John was a logical choice, but his morning radio program, "The Squirrel's Nest" was where he got most of his notoriety.

Then, as now, he went to elaborate lengths to prove a point if he knew he was right. Once he casually disregarded a note from the station auditor requesting twenty cents for an unauthorized long distance telephone call. Soon there was another note, then another and another, and finally it became too much for him. The next day a huge armored truck rolled up to the office. Two heavily-armed guards got out, marched into the bookkeeping offices, and requested to see the chief auditor.

"I'm sorry. He's not available right now. May I help you?"

"I have a certified check for twenty cents for him," the guard somberly informed the receptionist.

"I'll take it for him."

"I'm sorry. I'm not authorized to give it to you. He'll have to sign for it."

They refused to leave, waiting for the auditor to come out and sign for the twenty-cent check, which he finally did. The truck and guards had cost $25.00, over half John's weekly pay check. He made his point about the pettiness of management; what he didn't realize was that this particular accountant was not some isolated nit-picker. The same kinds of pettiness continue to hound him to this day; performers and executives just do not think alike—they never have and they never will. And to this day, John is amazed and infuriated with the seriousness with which businessmen regard small details and business routines, while, on the other hand, they can never seem to comprehend an entertainer's inability to explain exactly what it is that he does. The entertainer cannot explain it beyond assuring the business people that he will continue to perform if they will just leave him alone.

Jabbing the ribs of the well-padded has always been a Johnny favorite. He loves to play with commercials; businessmen hate him to play with their commercial spiels; and neither party can seem to see the other's side.

WOW had a local bank that advertised itself as the "Friendly Bank." John questioned exactly how friendly any bank is. Then one morning his listeners were treated to a commercial for the "Friendly Bank" that ended with, ". . . so stop in anytime, two, three in the morning. It's OK. We're the friendly bank. Help yourself, just leave a note."

"Not very funny!" said the bank president.

"He threatened to pull his advertising off the air. Not very funny at all!" said the station manager.

Johnny failed to see how anyone could take his comments as anything but a joke. Most of Omaha took it as a joke. But the bank president didn't and John went back to straight reading of the advertising copy.

One thing John didn't read straight was the open-ended interviews the record companies would send out for the D.J.'s in the sticks. These "open-ended" interviews are, in actuality, a recorded series of answers to questions the D.J. supposedly is asking the performer. A script comes with the recorded answers and as the questions are read off the script, an engineer plays the corresponding reply from the record.

An interview with Patti Page might go something like this:

> *Read from the script*: "Tell me, Patti, when did you first start performing?"
>
> *Reply from the record*: "When I was six, I used to get up at church socials and do it. I was considered quite unusual for a child of six."
>
> "And you first started performing professionally, when?"
>
> "Oh, the first time I ever got any money for it was from a group of neighborhood kids out in our garage. I did a whole show, everything."

John would get on the air without the script, or with a script of his own that would ask questions like: "I understand you're hitting the bottle pretty good, Patti. When did you first start?"

"When I was six I used to get up at church socials . . ."

You get the general idea. He would go on with questions about the star's sexual habits and anything else that popped into his mind.

It was not long before WOW Omaha was taken off the mailing list for open-ended interviews.

It seems as if everyone who was in Omaha at the time of Johnny's broadcasts has a favorite "Johnny" stunt he fondly remembers. He was definitely becoming a big fish and the only thing that was wrong was the size of the pond.

"I knew that I could never go very far as long as I stayed in Nebraska. The action and the opportunities were all either in New York or California."

A salary of $150 a week was not looking like so much of a pipe dream to someone who had already conquered Omaha. Today Omaha; tomorrow the world. Well, at least Los Angeles.

John got a cameraman friend of his to come in after working hours and, using WOW's equipment and film, they shot a one-half hour audition film for Johnny to take with him on his upcoming California vacation. The film showed Johnny doing a little bit of everything the versatile young performer could do. It had the magic and bits with "Eddie," his ventriloquist's dummy, as well as comedy monologues, interviews, news, weather, and station breaks.

His 1951 summer vacation rolled around and Johnny was ready. "I packed the wife and kids in our beat-up Olds with a U-Haul trailer, and we took off for California."

His half-hour audition film riding on the seat next to him like a golden ticket to the big time, they headed for San Francisco.

No need to unpack. "I knocked at every radio and TV door; at most of them, I couldn't even get inside."

"No openings, sorry."

37

JOHNNY CARSON

This was the first real professional rejection John had ever encountered. They did not treat him as a fellow Nebraskan, an Omaha celebrity, no less. He was just one more kid from the provinces trying to crack a tough nut.

With Jody, the kids, the beat-up Olds, U-Haul in tow, they headed south, looking like characters from *The Grapes of Wrath.* To the south was Hollywood and Los Angeles, places built on the firm foundations of fantasy and dreams. Certainly, here they would be more receptive to a young entertainer full of dreams, full of the raw material to turn out entertainment, the city's biggest export.

He hit every door again. The answers were the same, with minor variations. "No. Sorry, we aren't seeing any new performers. We'll let you know."

The future did not look too good. There was no point in looking for an apartment if he could not find work. John was not going to sling hash or pump gas waiting for the big break. He was a broadcaster; too many others had fallen into that trap and were still pumping gas at sixty-five years old, waiting for the big break. He had a job doing what he wanted in Omaha, and if worse came to worse, he could always go back.

It looked like that was where he was headed. His vacation time was running out and still no job was in sight when he got a call from an old childhood friend, Bill Brennan, who had gone into radio sales in Los Angeles. He had recommended Johnny to radio station KNXT.

Knowing that this was the last chance he had this time around, John was ready. He took the film and had an audition and interview which he thought had gone pretty well.

Feigning confidence he waited coolly for the word from the station. Finally it came. "Sorry, no openings at this time, but we'll definitely keep you in mind for anything in the future."

Sure!

Once again, he packed it all up, put it in the Olds, and started on the long ride back to Omaha.

Everyone has made a trip back home after one defeat or another, analyzing what went right and what went wrong. For most, it is a subway ride or a short commute, and then to

38

bed and on with the rest of life. For John, it was a long ride over half a continent with his own disappointment. Mile after endless mile on which to build new resolve, think of new ways to crack the big nut; mile after mile of planning.

Seldom caught unprepared, he must have spent a few of those miles deciding what he was going to tell those who knew he had been headed to seek fame and fortune.

A performer is by himself at times like these; there is nothing anyone, no matter how close they are, can say. He either knows how good he is and what he can do to make himself better, or he becomes a very bitter life insurance salesman.

John knew; besides, what he was going back to was not all that bad. He was something of a celebrity in Omaha by now. "The Squirrel's Nest" was more popular than ever. He was opening supermarkets and doing all the other hoopla local radio personalities specialize in. It was still a small pond, but John was getting to be a bigger and bigger fish.

Throwing himself wholeheartedly into his work at WOW, he was determined to be better prepared next time he took a shot at the big time. But for now, John was intent on giving Omaha the best he had.

Working for midwestern radio stations can get frightfully tedious: reading soy bean and corn quotes from the commodity markets, weather reports, and awfully dull local news. Anything to liven it up was fodder for John.

When he read that the *U.S.S.* "Missouri" had gone aground on a mud flat outside Hampton Roads, Virginia and the Navy, so far, was unable to get it off, John ran a contest for the best solution to the problem. The contest was a success and got a good play in Omaha, where the answers came from people who had spent most of their lives on top of tractors. This gave John some of the best material he had ever gotten. He was beginning to formulate bits and pieces of his low-keyed approach to broadcast comedy, taking lines from contestants and transposing a word or two here and there. He began to work off other peoples' follies and foibles, always keeping it topical.

While in the middle of the *U.S.S.* "Missouri" contest one

39

day, he was handed a slip of paper. "Secretary of the Navy Francis P. Mathews is waiting to see you."

Johnny read the note to himself and then leaned into the microphone. "I've just been told by one of my staff that Mr. Francis Mathews, Secretary of the Navy, is waiting to see me." Then turning to the man who gave him the note, he said, "Good. You tell him to get that boat off the mud and report back to me in twenty minutes!"

He closed up the show that morning and walked out of the studio to find a very well-dressed, middle-aged man waiting to see him.

"Hello, I'm Francis Mathews and I've been listening to the contest you've been running."

Johnny swallowed hard. "Yes?"

The Secretary liked it; so did almost everyone else in Omaha. Johnny was their boy and he had the good manners to poke fun at battleships in the Atlantic, crazies lying on California's Pacific beaches, pigeons, and banks.

Always aware of who his audience was, he never assaulted them, pointing out their own foibles. Instead, he aimed at targets farther away or universally disliked, making it easier to tune in because listeners knew they were not going to bear the brunt of the joke.

With his family but not his salary growing along with his reputation, John continued the after hours magic and ventriloquism to help defray the costs of two young sons and a wife.

One night after a hard evening mystifying the Elks, he was greeted at the door by his wife. She could barely control herself enough to get the words out.

"You got a long distance telephone call from Los Angeles. You're to call operator number 46 as soon as you get in."

"It's pretty late. Maybe I'd better wait till tomorrow?"

Jody was practically jumping up and down by now. "They said it didn't matter how late; besides, there's two hours difference!"

He went to the phone and calmly picked it up, showing none of his excitement, or fear that it might not be what he hoped. "Operator number 46 in Los Angeles, please."

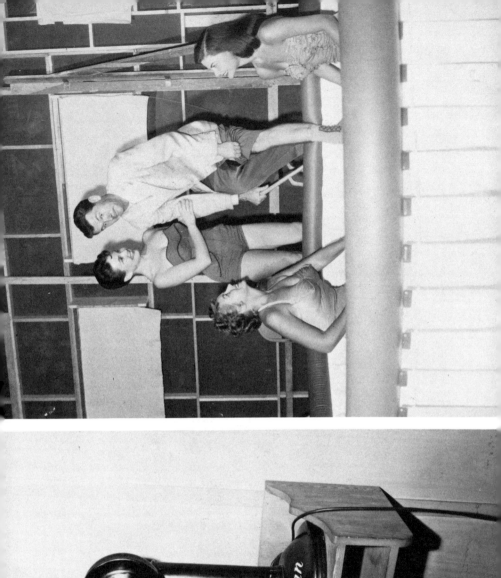

"Is it one of the radio stations?" Jody asked.

"If I knew that, I wouldn't have to call, would I?" John answered her.

The scratchy, sometimes interrupted voice, from far away finally said, "Hello. Is that you, John?" It was Bill Brennan. "I've got some good news for you." He paused for what seemed an eternity. "There's a staff announcer's job opening here at KNXT and it's yours if you want it. The pay is not the biggest, $135 a week, but you can make do on it, I think."

"That's fantastic, Bill. Can I let you know in the morning on this? I'd like to take a night to think about it." They talked a while longer and John hung up to go through the motions of making a decision.

John was now becoming a not-so-small-sized Omaha celebrity. He could stick it out in the midwest a while longer until he had a real solid platform from which to make the big jump, or he could throw caution overboard and take one giant stride toward the big time.

He and Jody talked it over late into the night, but there could not have been much doubt in his mind; the opportunities were definitely limited in Omaha.

At eight o'clock the next morning he was on the phone to the West Coast. Poor Bill Brennan.

"God, John, it's not even six in the morning out here!"

"I'm sorry. I forgot about that. I'll take it."

The cobwebs still in his head, Bill frantically tried to figure out what he was talking about. "What?"

"The staff announcer's job. I'm on my way."

The decrepit Oldsmobile got its last good tune-up before heading for that junk yard in the sky. The U-Haul was packed for the last time. Jody would stay behind this time to tie up the family affairs while John started work and found a place for them to live.

Finally, it was all in, on, or behind the Olds. Johnny Carson kissed his wife and children, eased his cargo out onto the open road, and left Nebraska.

He was not four bars into "California, Here I Come" when the first tire blew on the car. He got out, unhitched the trailer, opened the trunk, and changed the tire. It took almost an hour. By the time he finally arrived, all the tires had blown at least once; practice makes perfect, and by now he had beaten that hour's time by a long shot. Actually, the entire trip was something less than a good omen. Everything that could happen, did. He got snowed in during a blizzard in Oklahoma, Texas had the worst cold spell in its history, and the Death Valley crossing had John warily eyeing the skeletons littering the roadside.

In Los Angeles he stayed with Jody's aunt while he checked into work and looked for a new place to live. His mind was fully occupied with the newness of everything at KNXT, but finally with a little help he found a duplex apartment in the Toluca Lake area. He wired Omaha and soon the family were on their way.

At KNXT John was now the station announcer, which meant he was right back where he started at WOW two years before this, except this time there weren't any of the friendly "howdys" from fellow Nebraskans. Here everyone was under the gun, and they watched whom they said what to. Locked up tight, that was the way it was, and John felt the pressure.

"Boy, I'll tell you, it's a big change when you're the new man at a station, fresh out of Omaha. You feel shut out of everything."

He was back to sweeping out the announcer's booth, reading the weather, time, and station identification. If the situation looked the same that was all right, he had worked this way off the bottom rung before. John knew he would do it again.

"He was intensely serious about succeeding," one television executive who remembers him then says. "A very nice, easy person to deal with, understanding that anyone who's shooting for the big pot has a driving nervousness and inner tension. Considering that drive, Johnny was as pleasant and nice as a kid could be. But he was never somebody you could feel a complete kinship with."

John felt locked out because he was not a "somebody" yet. There was not too much time for "kinship," he was too busy getting himself farther up that ladder.

42

John knew, or at least thought he knew, what was at the top of the ladder. Every night when he got out of his car at his duplex, he could look directly above his little apartment and see the homes of the stars nestled in snug alcoves on the mountainsides overlooking the valley. He would always stop for a moment. "I used to say, Bob Hope lives right over there."

It is doubtful that Hope looked down the mountainside at his future neighbor, but in Johnny's mind, he was already "just dropping by to borrow a cup of vodka, Bob."

Events began to move in a predictable pattern, as they so often do for people willing to put in the extra hours and extra discipline of hard work. He moved out of the staff announcer's booth and into regularly scheduled programs. He began to break in with occasional on-camera commercials and local spot announcing.

Now D.J.'ing on a pretty regular basis, he spent every available moment working on his next project. "While the record was playing, I was sitting there in the booth putting together ideas for my own TV show."

He would always have his antennae out whenever walking down halls or in the parking lot, trying to corner any of the executives and tell them about his show idea.

"There's a Johnny Carson here to see you, Mr. Andrews."

"Johnny who?"

Anybody who's made it in the industry says the same thing: "It ain't easy!"

Prepared, John would start his pitch. "I know you're a busy man, sir, so I won't take too much of your time."

Executive replies are usually the same. "Busy isn't the word for it."

"Yes, sir."

After shuffling a few more papers the executive would look up. "What's the problem, Carson."

"No problem, sir. I've been working on an idea for a new television show and I'd . . ."

"The last fifty people through that door had an idea for a new television show," reaching for his intercom button.

43

"Frankly, Carson, I haven't got the time right now. Cynthia, have you got the revised scheduling for . . .."

Ultimately he talked some local CBS television executives into an audition. His show was to be low-keyed and satirical sketches, bits of odd-ball humor, and off-beat guests when they could be found for nothing.

Generally, they liked the idea. What sold them on it was the budget: $25.00 a show. That is the kind of language executives understand! Johnny got an extra $50.00 a week for doing the show which aired locally in the Los Angeles area on Sunday afternoons for a one-half hour.

"Carson's Cellar" was the title, and indeed it was Carson's. John did virtually everything, with the exception of running the cameras and tape recorders. He wrote all the scripts himself using any available time to jot down ideas and thoughts.

"Here's Peggy Lee's latest . . .."

Out would come the pads and pencils. During lunch breaks he would race down to the secretarial pool, steal a typewriter, and frantically type the script for the coming Sunday. Then, racing back to the booth, he would spin the records again.

The next day it was the same thing, except this time it was the mimeograph machine. On many days he would still be wiping that horrible blue duplicating ink from his hands and clothes as he sat down at the microphone again.

He always got it done, sometimes with seconds to spare, but come Sunday afternoon, the kid who had filled Johnny's spot as staff announcer would somberly intone, "KNXT cautiously presents 'Carson's Cellar.' "

John had made himself a promise when he left Nebraska. "If I didn't have my own show after a year, I was going to move on to New York. I was never one who believed in waiting for the breaks," John explained.

One year—that was what he had allowed himself and that was what it took. There aren't many people naive enough to set that kind of unattainable goal for themselves; still fewer could beat the deadline.

The show came off well. It was a blend of all different types of comedy, much as the first half hour of the "Tonight

Show" is today. In the trade papers the reviews were good: "Bright . . . newcomer with lots of possibilities . . . someone to watch."

Johnny began to see his name crop up from time to time in the columns of the morning papers that Hollywood devours with its breakfast. His stardom was ascending.

On the show one zany stunt followed another. With only that $25.00 to spend, most of the show was the result of John's brain, which CBS was getting for $50.00. But with no money, guests were hard to come by, so once John had a production assistant walk past the camera. As the blur passed, Johnny identified it. "That was my guest for today, Red Skelton."

The man crossed so fast that there was no way anyone could tell whether it was Red or not. One person who knew for sure it was not Red was Skelton himself, who regularly tuned in every Sunday.

The next Sunday the guest on "Carson's Cellar" really was Red Skelton. Red told Johnny that he had a good-sized following among Los Angeles's show business community, a fact which was still quite unbeknown to John. Jack Benny and Fred Allen were devotees, as well as Groucho and Jerry Lewis, many of whom began making guest appearances.

More newsprint in the trade papers translated to more viewers, and that meant advertisers. In true Southern California tradition, "Carson's Cellar's" first sponsor was a local used car dealer.

It was fast becoming the "in" program to catch if you were in the business. Johnny was good and his own material was good, so it was not too much of a surprise when occasionally he would tune in one of the prime time variety shows and see some of his material going over very well to a national audience. After all, how many people are watching TV on Sunday afternoons in Los Angeles? Johnny was doing a lot of writing for a lot of big names and getting $50.00 a week for the effort.

Somebody over at NBC must have known where the material was coming from because a producer of one of the huge all-star revues, so much in style back then, after much

JOHNNY CARSON

effort, managed to get John on the phone. "I've been trying to reach you for over two weeks. Who's your agent?"

Johnny replied quite innocently, "I haven't got one."

In short order, the William Morris Agency snapped him up in their 10 percent jaws.

What NBC wanted was one of his sketches for the revue, which he did, to excellent notices.

The right people, or the wrong people, depending on your point of view, were watching. They offered John a network show, "Earn Your Vacation."

Dreamt up in the men's room at Los Angeles airport, everyone involved with the show (or "that little atrocity," as John calls it) from the producer, director, and cameraman, all the way through the viewers and studio audience, agreed that the best thing to happen in TV that year was when they finally flushed "the little atrocity" away. The only mystery was why it had not flushed away in the airport before it had a chance to spread.

John was working himself half to death, but it was beginning to pay dividends. The big name viewers, as well as borrowing an occasional line, were also touting him to the different network brass. Very few people said "Johnny who?" any more.

After a run of little less than a year, "Carson's Cellar" went off the air. Skelton, one of his original fans, was quick to snap him up and put him on his staff as a comedy writer.

On Red's staff John flourished. Not only did he and Skelton get on well, but John had the knack so few comedy writers possess: the ability to write material another personality was to deliver.

John Carson however, is, was, and always will be a performer, not a writer. His ego requires it; it is a necessary food for the animal.

Soon the performer began to reemerge. Red began using him in the show for occasional bits here and there, and everyone who worked on the staff was treated to an endless stream of Carson gags, humor, and magic backstage.

So when the telephone call came, it could not have been that much of a shock; but still, the entire affair did smack of

46

a plot from a 1940's Judy Garland movie, as Jody called John to the phone.

"It's the show. Something happened to Red," she said, handing the receiver to John.

"Yeah?"

"How fast can you get here, John? Never mind that. Just get in the car and get here fast. You have to go on, Red's been hurt."

John had been working around the house and was filthy. "What happened? Is it serious?"

There was no concealing the panic coming from the studio. "We don't know yet. He ran into a door and knocked himself cold. He's still out." The concern for Red was only momentary. "Forget that! Just get your ass in the car and get down here!"

In true show business tradition, the show must go on, especially if someone like Ford Motor Company is paying several million dollars to see to it.

Johnny dropped the receiver and raced for the bathroom. In Clark Kent tradition he was shaved, showered, and dressed in moments. It was not until he was racing at breakneck speed to get to the studio, some sixty minutes away, that he began to think what he was going to do once he got there.

Frantically, he began dredging his years as an entertainer to find the material for the show. He discarded any thoughts of magic or ventriloquism. This was big time, network prime time, comedy. A shot at the pot of gold. Tonight was the night Johnny Carson would show that he could deliver with the best of them.

Red had been rehearsing a comedy bit that required him to run through a breakaway door. In Skelton fashion, he attacked it with his usual frenetic commitment, except the door did not give and Red was out for a full two hours.

When John raced into the studio, air time was minutes away and Red had just then begun to woozily come around; there was no question, Johnny would have to go on.

Frantic producers trying desperately to keep the ulcer under control raced up to him. "Are you ready? This is network prime time, Johnny, there are millions out there

47

watching. . . . Now just take it easy. You're going to be great. Are you sure you're ready?"

Wanting as much as he did to be as big a star as Red, Johnny must have fantasized this moment a thousand times; every performer does. But with Johnny's abhorrence of the unexpected, rather than dream about the general moment, John probably envisioned most of the details. Ready? If there's one thing Johnny Carson always is, it is ready.

"Entertainment is like any other major industry; it's cold, big business. The business end wants to know one thing: can you do the job? If you can, you're in, you're made; if you can't, you're out."

When the show went off the air that night, Johnny Carson was in. He had taken the country. The reviews were good. Now everyone in the industry was talking about the bright new talent.

Within sixty days, CBS had shot a pilot, liked it, and signed him to his own half hour show to start in the summer of that year, 1955. It was aired on Thursday evenings at ten o'clock and was called "The Johnny Carson Show."

"I built the show initially around a format of low-keyed skits and commentary on topical subjects . . . something rather like the 'Tonight Show.' "

Actually, it was more like "The George Gobel Show," which was then at its height of popularity.

The reviews were, for the most part, good. They liked Johnny and his delivery, and thought he was pleasant and warm; but the rest of the show was knocked for what it was, a copy of Gobel. After praising Johnny's stand-up routines and tongue-in-cheek remarks, the *New York Times* went on to say, "The rest of the show, unfortunately, was only too typical summer video fare . . . a routine girl vocalist, a conventional jazz unit, and a sketch about a guest who did not know when to go home." The article closed by urging CBS to put more effort into the show because, "He would seem worth the investment."

, The show aired opposite "The Lux Video Theater" and despite the generally favorable response, it did not draw the viewers. CBS was unwilling to settle for a part of the market.

They wanted all of it and John was not keeping enough people away from "Lux" for CBS, so they called him in to talk about it.

Ben Brady, the show's producer, took Johnny out to lunch to break the bad news to him. Crowded restaurants are good places for that type of thing, nobody dares scream and yell with all those people around.

"John, we're not coming up with the right numbers on the weekly Neilsens and I think I know where you're going wrong."

"Where?"

"The show isn't important enough."

"What?"

Brady took a long drag on his cigarete. "Let me see if I can expand on that. What the show needs is a feeling of importance. Do you understand what I'm talking about now?"

"No."

Becoming exasperated with Johnny's inability to use the executive portion of his brain, he gave him the ultimatum. "You're going to have to make it important, John."

"How?"

Nobody to this day has answered that question, but if a copy of George Gobel didn't work, how about a copy of Jackie Gleason?

Johnny tried to continue with his own brand of light humor, like betting the audience he could keep their attention riveted to the stage by doing nothing but an elementary tap dance routine. No one's eyes left him as he carefully tapped out an innocuous "Tea For Two" number in front of a giant screen showing atomic bomb blasts, fireworks, battleships, God creating the world, and other things.

Nice. But not good enough for Jello, the show's sponsor. They stepped in and demanded a say in the show's content. Naively believing in the good intentions of everyone, John let them do as they pleased with the show.

He had started out on a nice note of honesty when he brought Jody and his children (three boys by now, Kit, four, Ricky, two, and Corey, one), on the first show and explained that Virginia Gibson was just an actress who would play his wife on the show, but as the show began to grind toward the end of its contracted thirty-nine weeks, all semblance of honesty vanished with the fog rising from the sets of new and lavish production numbers.

The newspapers began to say things like, "Thirty minutes of chuckles are free of screams. . . . Impertinence in a minor key . . . etc."

Jello wanted thirty minutes of screams free of chuckles and began to dictate, along with CBS, who Johnny's guests would be. They began to rewrite scripts without his knowledge.

"They hired me because I was great; then everyone had an idea for improving it."

It began to look like the Los Angeles freeway in the production offices as writers and directors came and went, all trying to make Johnny Carson "important."

Johnny always plays his cards tight to the vest. Aware of those who made it to a national platform and burned themselves out through overexposure (Gobel and Sid Caesar are excellent examples), he would talk at great length about the need for television performers conserving their talents to last them through an entire career. Yet, here he had hardly even been exposed and he was watching the whole thing slide down Carnak's "Calcutta Camode."

"It was primarily through my own naivete that the show failed. . . . I let them start telling me what to do," John explains.

There was not much to tell him. Practically the entire show was written by CBS and Jello; all Johnny did was show up and stand out there in front of the cameras so there would be no question as to whose fault it was.

"They told me they were going to make the show important and did it with chorus girls. The girls would scream, 'And here's the star of our show, Johnny Carson!' and I'd come bouncing through a curtain of balloons. I don't know if we were ever important, but we could match anybody in pretentiousness."

Mercifully the thirty-nine weeks of the contract ended and

"The Johnny Carson Show" quietly left the airwaves.

Ben Brady delivered the eulogy. "He didn't have the power. He is generally not a strong stand-up comedian. Johnny is bright, very inventive, and very funny, but he's low key." He didn't go on to elaborate on exactly what his contributions to the show had been.

The supercharged pace came to a screeching halt; the revolving door in the production offices, which had resulted in no less than eight different writers and seven different directors, stopped turning, and "The Johnny Carson Show" slid from view. Everyone knew whose fault it was, including John.

The rocket ride to the top was over. It fell short and landed him back at his home in Encino. "That was my first *big* lesson. That's where I learned that if you don't keep control, you're going to bomb out, and there's nobody to blame but yourself."

Fortunately John had been as careful of overextending himself financially as well as artistically. When he had landed the big show, he had not made any changes in his life style; he was still living in Encino and driving a '52 Chevrolet. Jody was driving a '51 Ford. The damage was mostly to his ego. But where else can you hurt a performer?

News travels faster through the show business community than anywhere else in the world. Rona Barrett can be on TV every night with gossip no more than twenty-four hours old, but by the time she gets in front of the cameras, it is no longer news to anyone in the business.

Those deadly beacons that broadcast the news to the remotest reaches of the theatrical world were working fine when "The Johnny Carson Show" made its farewell appearance.

"Carson is out!"

"Johnny Carson flopped. . . . You should have heard the sound he made when he hit the floor."

"On that bit for the special, forget Carson."

"He's out. . . . Dead!"

"Johnny who?"

John was still under contract to CBS, but it did not take the most perceptive person in the world to see that CBS had no intention of taking another gamble with John Carson. He placed a few perfunctory calls and went in to talk about his future with CBS several times, but it did not look good.

"We're looking into several properties for you, John," he would be told. Lighting cigarettes and looking at the ceiling, they were always careful not to look him in the eye. "The problem is in finding something that fits your unique talents. We don't want to make the same mistake again. Another thing is scheduling. You're not Thursday night material. No, I think if we can find you something on Sundays, late, that's more your audience."

Never being one not to recognize where he is not wanted, he would smile that "I'm on to your act so why do we have to go through this charade" smile of his, turn, and head back to Jody and the boys in Encino where he waited the calls from his agency, William Morris.

Ten percent of nothing is just that, nothing. A client on the books who is not working is worthless to a talent agency. It pays them to do everything possible to get him working again. Every Nebraska kid knows that good agents get out there and stump for their clients—keep them working fifty-two weeks a year if they want to.

John kept waiting for that phone to ring.

After all, they had told him they could get him jobs and that was the reason he should sign with them. They were going to help him with his career . . . well, weren't they?

Still the phone did not ring. Finally, John climbed into the old Chevy and went down to see them.

"Look, I can get myself some kind of an act together. Get a couple of writers to work with me," he told them.

With the eternal talent agent smile on their faces, they told him, "Sorry Johnny, we can't do that."

"Why not? I've done acts before. I've done everything there is to do in this industry. Let's get some people together and see if we can't at least latch onto some club dates. But for God's sake, let's not sit around doing nothing!"

Performers just don't understand what the business is like.

Agents do, however. "John, this cancellation thing has left a bad taste in everyone's mouth. Let's wait a month or two till it goes away, and then I'm sure we're going to have no trouble finding something for you."

"Two months?" The reaction he was getting totally stunned him. "What the hell are you talking about? I've got a wife and three kids, how do you propose I feed them while you wait for the time to be right?"

"Now don't get excited. This fall, spring at the very latest, we should have something for you. . . . A soap opera, maybe."

Hurt and enraged, he raced back to Encino and wrote the script for his club act himself; then he went out knocking on doors until he finally sold the idea to a place in Bakersfield called "Maison Jaussaud." The pay was $400 a week and no one took 10 percent.

After he had polished it, he invited the top men from William Morris to come out and see what he could do. They sent two junior executive types who sat in a corner, said nothing, and left as soon as the act was over.

He never heard another word from the William Morris agency until years later in New York when things were going very well and the future looked unlimited. They approached him once again to try to handle his career then.

"Here come this agency's top guys. Big deal! Old buddy-buddy. Let bygones be bygones; no hard feelings; let's forget the past." As Johnny tells the story today, it is obvious he never forgets. "They said, 'How about our representing you again? We've got it all figured out how to shoot you straight to the top.' I listened until they finished their spiel, and then I said, 'Thank you, no, gentlemen. Where were you when I needed you?' "

Johnny does not like agents, even those who are not doing anything wrong. He speaks of MCA, the now defunct giant talent agency who handled him in better times:

> I was doing fine, getting the treatment they call "servicing the client." I remember one day I was getting ready to leave their office to do the show, and this agency man makes moves to go with me. I asked him,

"What are you doing?" He said, "Don't you want me to go to the show with you?" I told him I thought I could make it myself. What I felt like telling him was, "You want to do something for me? Iron my shirts!"

Johnny *really* does not like agents.

After he made it to the "Tonight Show" Johnny was always inordinately proud that he was not a comedian from the mountains with all those "We were so poor . . .." jokes. He came from that great middleclass, midwest part of our world. What he never seems to acknowledge in his disparaging remarks about comedians from the street is that they know who an agent is and what he will do to you.

The poor Irish, Italian, and Jewish comics knew who the agent was from their first days on earth. He came to collect the rent. He loaned you money when you needed it. He spoke to old Mr. Klein about putting a different brand juke box in his candy store.

When these "We were so poor . . .." comedians walked into their first agent's office, no one had to identify the man on the other side of the desk.

They do not hate agents either. They never trusted them enough to hate them. Knowing that these men live off the work of other people, they merely recognize the species for what it is.

To this day, Johnny has trouble recognizing who people are and what their method of business is. It is much easier for him to stay locked up tight, away from the people who are going to use him, locked up tight, away from people he cannot recognize.

Supporting a family from a week or two in Bakersfield was not just hard, it was impossible. John used up what little savings he had and was now flat, stone broke. He had to wire his family for money to keep his family alive.

At this time, he met a man by the name of Al Bruno. Al Bruno was a manager, someone to stand between Johnny and all the agents, producers, network executives, and other people he was having trouble dealing with.

If a well-meaning, over-ambitious, boyish WASP with the

honesty of the great plains was to hire himself a paladin, about the best thing he could have done was to start off with a man like Al Bruno.

Johnny told Al of the treatment he had received at CBS and William Morris. Bruno nodded. He had heard the stories before. He did agree with the agents on one count though; the name Johnny Carson left a bad taste in casting people's mouths on the West Coast. Bruno moved him to New York where he was, for all practical purposes, a new commodity.

John was lucky in finding a bank that would loan him enough money, along with that which he had borrowed from his father, to make the shift to the East.

Once in New York, Al managed to keep Johnny busy, jumping from one guest shot to another. A week substituting for Robert Q. Lewis, and two days on "Password," etc. Hardly a show originating from New York was a stranger to Johnny.

Bruno got a press agent and Johnny began popping up in the columns. His reticence to speak nowadays is in marked contrast to the early years in New York. Hardly a week went by without Johnny having something to say about the climate of the industry.

"I don't think, for instance, that George Gobel is less amusing now than he was last year, but the ratings will prove me wrong," Johnny Carson said, talking about ratings, his (as well as so many others) personal Waterloo. His cryptic quotes became a regular feature of Earl Wilson and Leonard Lyons. "This season Gobel's opposition is a western called 'Gunsmoke.' What can Gobel do if some people like westerns?"

Johnny Carson does a dramatic role on "Playhouse 90." He does two weeks on "To Tell the Truth."

What do you think of the state of television comedy, John?

"It's almost impossible to do a live comedy show every week and keep people with you. Even if you've got the best material in the world, people get tired of looking at you."

"What's My Line?" "U.S. Steel Hour." He substitutes

a week for Paar. He is seen more than some people with their own shows.

The Friars, a theatrical club for nightclub and vaudeville performers, makes him a member, and Johnny's acid tongue becomes a regular at their roasts. It is very good exposure for John; there's hardly anyone in the industry who does not know him as a quick-witted, lightning-fast expert at the type of repertoire required for Friars' roasts, or required when you need someone to fill in on a moment's notice.

Don Fedderson, a West Coast producer, had been doing a filmed television show with Edgar Bergen entitled, "Do You Trust Your Wife?" Fedderson decided to move the show to New York, switch to a live format, and change the name and the star of the show. The new name was to be grammatically incorrect but "Who Do You Trust?" would be Johnny Carson's home for five years when he won an audition for the job of master of ceremonies and readily accepted.

"Who Do You Trust?" was a typical daytime quiz show which relied heavily, as so many do, on the contestants' abilities to embarrass or humiliate themselves in return for a Norge refrigerator/freezer. In the beginning, all the contestants were married or about to be. They would be selected from the studio audience, and then would come on for a brief chat with Johnny before trying for all the wonderful prizes.

With Johnny's exceptional ability to get a laugh out of the most improbable situation, the talk portion of the show was the only segment that showed any promise. Johnny would elicit the most double-entendré loaded answers from his unsuspecting guests, and then, always with the look of a minister's son, he would drop remarks that, coming from a less wholesome face, could get you banned from the airwaves for life.

Soon he found that the odder the guest, the better the interview went. Two brothers who were both undertakers were considered pretty normal.

Fedderson soon saw the light too, and he gave John an open hand in revamping the show. The quiz portion was always kept as the hub around which the rest revolved, but as the shows rolled past the interviews began to dominate them. It must have been the right decision because by the time "Who Do You Trust?" went off the air it was the highest rated show on daytime television and ABC's best rated show of all, with a religiously regular daily audience of over five and one-half million.

Five days a week "Who Do You Trust?" went out to the public, but still Bruno kept placing John on a variety show here and a panel show there. He emceed the Miss Universe Pageant.

Johnny Carson roasts Garry Moore at the Friars.
"What do you think of the state of television comedy, John?"
He could not say enough to the press. "A comedy performer should not be on television more than six to ten times a year after he's established."

Johnny has a medium on "Who Do You Trust?" and she holds a seance. There's no time for everything on the show. Out go the close-ups of lawn mowers and matched luggage; out goes anything that will give him less time with the guests —more talk, less quiz.

"Find those odd balls!" the cry goes out from the production offices who have long since learned that for the most part, the studio audience is composed of dullards. The more they want to get on the show, the duller they are. Every day the staff combs the newspapers, magazines, the street, anywhere, looking for the guest Johnny can play off.

"You mean you don't wash with water?"
"That's right, Johnny. I cleanse myself with air baths."
The nose wrinkles. He sniffs the air, and the audience loves it. "Exactly how do you go about taking an air bath?"
Deadly serious the man explains. "First I get totally undressed, then I lay down in front of an open window

57

and let the cleansing air flow over my entire body. Then I turn over and do the other side."

"I see." Here it comes. "I suppose if you want a shower, you stand in front of a fan?"

Perfect! It brings down the house. A beautiful ad lib moment. Or was it?

Each guest goes through a careful screening process where the staff ascertains exactly what and where entertainment possibilities are for this guest. Then a script is prepared for John, showing areas of potential conversation in which the contestants have been coached.

Johnny replaces Tom Ewell for two months in the Broadway comedy "Tunnel Of Love." He plays opposite Marsha Hunt for one month at the National Theater, then moves with the show to the Martin Beck Theatre to complete the run.

He replaces Paar for two weeks in the summer and is criticized for allowing the stars too much freedom and losing control of the show.

Chapter Four

"To Tell The Truth." "What's My Line?" "The Garry Moore Show." Does Johnny Carson ever stop?

When asked what he thinks about television comedy, John answered, "I couldn't be happier than I am right here on daytime television. I'm quite happy with my little audience of five million. I'll tell you something else, I've got the best writers in the world coming right out of the studio audience. ... I don't need fifteen writers coming up with bad gags week after week." Johnny Carson never forgets. "It's not like nighttime television where you don't have any control. ... The boys upstairs take over and then when things go sour, they blame it on the performer."

The new word for this era is overexposure, but it does not seem to apply to Johnny. People know they just saw him last night, but they can't quite remember if it was on "To Tell The Truth" or "Truth or Consequences."

The press, who originally had hailed him as a bright new-comer, suddenly rediscovered him. Always a serious student of the performing arts, John wrote a column on television comedy for the *Herald Tribune*.

"You're a comedian when you come out and stand in front of an audience and be funny," he said in it. Sounds simple. If it were we would all do it for a living.

Then John took over for Paar for two weeks again in the summer, then back to his own bailywick.

"... but you've got to breathe through your nose or mouth, or you'll suffocate!"

"That's a common misconception, John. With practice you can learn to breathe through your toes. Here, let me show you. . . ."

It becomes a little-known fact outside of the industry, but Johnny Carson is running the dirtiest show ever aired. The same way he presently uses that little boy "who me?" grin to breeze questionable material past the censors on the "Tonight Show," he used it on "Who Do You Trust?", except there were no censors then, so everything went out to the bored housewives, and they loved it.

Johnny was earning somewhere in the vicinity of $50,000 a year for "Who Do You Trust?" plus whatever he made for his innumerable guest appearances. He was driving a Porsche and living with Jody and the kids in Harrison, New York, an upper middleclass suburb of New York City. Harrison is wealthy, but not extravagant as John was still being careful not to overextend himself. He had learned his lesson and now knew how fast it could all evaporate.

He was becoming too big for daytime television and the scripts for prime time situation comedies began to flood into his office. He turned them all down for one reason or another. Mostly, because they required him to play a bloodless, spineless, simpering midwestern husband—definitely not where he was headed.

"My specialty is light satire of the very relaxed school. I have a feeling that it's the one form of comedy that will survive on TV," said John.

Then the question was raised of a talk show for Johnny on ABC. That rumor was good for at least two months. When that petered out, the word was that "Who Do You Trust?" would go nighttime, late, opposite Paar. It never moved. But Johnny did.

He flew to London to emcee a Paul Anka special, and when he returned, Paar was in trouble with NBC; or NBC was in trouble with Paar, depending on whom you listened to. Because he had done well substituting for Jack, John's name was among those being thrown around, for it was becoming obvious that Paar's days were numbered on the "Tonight Show."

More Friars roasts. More panels. More variety specials. No, Virginia, Johnny Carson does not ever stop.

In January of 1962, the situation was getting out of hand as Jack Paar nightly began to bleed all over the tube. The first reliable rumors began to circulate that Johnny was the logical choice.

"It was NBC that came up with the offer for me to replace Paar permanently. I turned it down, cold; not many people know that. I just wasn't sure I could cut it," he said.

He had second thoughts, though. Things had changed since the first "Johnny Carson Show." Sponsors were willing to settle for a part of the audience now. Three of the bigger shows on television ran opposite each other on Sunday nights: "Maverick," "The Ed Sullivan Show," and "The Steve Allen Show."

His rejection of the NBC offer got a very definite reaction from his manager. "What the hell are you talking about!" Al Bruno didn't think he was not ready. "You gotta be kidding. This is the chance of a lifetime!"

"If you're ready for it," was Johnny's reply.

Bruno could barely control himself. "Who the hell is better prepared?" Johnny was not buying, so he went on, "There's no one, and I mean *no one* who handles a television interview better than you. Every day of the week, you're doing exactly the same thing as the 'Tonight Show,' except you're doing it with housewives instead of stars!"

"Al, it's not just changing jobs. There's a hell of a lot of difference between a half hour daily quiz show and an hour and forty-five minutes every night," he told him.

Everybody came to him with advice. Take it. Don't take it. Take it and I'll tell you how to run it. In the end, John turned it down.

Meanwhile, at NBC the situation with Paar was deteriorating at an accelerating pace. The fuse to that giant block of uniquely Paar explosive had less than an inch to go, but it was not a steady burn; it sputtered and flickered every now and then, and with each sputter the phones began to ring. The sponsors wanted to know what would happen if Jack left.

"He's not going to leave!"
"But if he does?"
"Jack has personally assured me that he is happy here at NBC."
"But if he leaves who will replace him?"
"We have a number of people under consideration."
"Who?"

Who indeed! It was a well-known fact in New York at that time that NBC had "talked to everyone except Albert Schweitzer," including Groucho, Steve, Merv, Bob Newhart, Jackie Gleason, and of course, Joey. Most merely turned down the opportunity to try and follow Paar's act. Those that said they would be happy to take some of NBC's money for the privilege of what was then considered certain death either wanted too much of NBC's lucre, or would obviously be unable to hold the impressive list of sponsors Paar had built up over the last five years.

They kept throwing names around Rockefeller Center until Paar finally set March 29 as the last day NBC could expect him to hold down the desk on the "Tonight Show." Now the names really began to fly.

In the end though, the name of Carson kept popping out as one of the few men NBC could get who had the necessary skills to do the job. He proved daily that he could think on his feet. He had considerable skills from his many performing endeavors. But what weighed heavier in his favor than anything else was his background in radio broadcasting, where the man in front of the microphone had to keep it moving above all else. Silence on the air is like blank pages in a book.

Both Steve Allen and Paar had that same radio experience in which they constantly kept their eyes on the studio clock, watched the script, cued up the records, made sure they left enough time for a late arriving interview, and did not forget to sweep up and lock the studio.

As Mort Werner, then programming boss at NBC said, "All we're asking is that he devote his entire life to the program."

Once again NBC picked up the phone and called Carson. They told him how right he was for the job, how much they liked him, what his unique qualifications were, and then they told him what it would be like doing the "Tonight Show."

"What do I need that for?" Johnny still wasn't buying. "Why me?"

"Because you're about the only person who can do it. We've got $15 million a year in advertising and you're one of the very few people in the entertainment industry today who we feel can keep them."

Honesty always did appeal to John. "Can you give me some time to think on it?"

"How much time?" NBC didn't have a lot of time. The minute the word went out that Paar was leaving, sponsors started cancelling anything due to air after the March 29 cut-off date.

"Two weeks," John replied.

NBC agreed. They would have preferred two minutes, but that simply was not going to be the case. Johnny Carson had never jumped into anything unprepared, and he was not about to jump into this without all the facts.

Very few television performers are ever as secure as Johnny was on "Who Do You Trust?" He had just begun his fifth year and was a legitimate star of daytime television, with a rabid following of bored housewives who daily looked forward to his deft double entendrés and slightly risqué jokes.

But things were changing. All was not honey and cream in Harrison, New York. Jody was beginning to make moves in the direction of the door, and Johnny began to think that this might be the time for him to make a move.

The regular paycheck from ABC was good but, "I got to thinking. Sure I could remain secure in daytime TV and not run the risk of failure. But there's something more to show business than security. I suppose it's ego. But what you want most is recognition from other performers as well as the public. You don't get that on daytime TV."

The sigh of relief that went up at NBC programming offices when Johnny said he'd do the show could be heard all the way to New Jersey. Advertising salesmen for the "Tonight Show" raced to their phones to assure their remaining clients that all was well in Tonightland.

Mort Werner was the happiest. He had very good feelings about Johnny. "When can you start, John?" Mort asked.

"It depends on when ABC will let me out of my contract. There shouldn't be any trouble though."

It wasn't really ABC who said no to Johnny, it was the producer of "Who Do You Trust?", Don Fedderson. When Johnny broke the big news to ABC, they said it was OK, but as soon as he left they were going to cancel "Who Do You Trust?"

Fedderson pleaded with the network. He could get a replacement. How could they just throw away their highest rated show, he wanted to know.

ABC's position was clear. It was Carson, not Fedderson's format for a quiz show that kept five and one-half million women ironing in front of the TV.

Fedderson's decision was strictly a financial one. If he was out of a job the minute Johnny and "Who Do You Trust?" left ABC, then he would insist that Carson's contract be fulfilled, so he could stick it out for another six months.

This was an unexpected turn of events and it could very well have queered the entire deal. Johnny had Bruno call and break the news to NBC, which he did, coming back to John with the news he wanted to hear.

NBC would wait the six months, filling in with guest celebrities until Johnny's obligations with ABC were fulfilled.

Most often, when a performer wants to break a contract in order to make a giant jump, the networks will not hold him or will let him out after a reasonable sum is agreed upon for a buy-out. The reason for this is performers' nasty habit of making a shambles of the show they have been doing until the network finally lets them go.

The contract with "Who Do You Trust?" did not have that long to run, so Johnny would not have to resort to that kind of trickery, but he was none too pleased with Fedderson and ABC, and he began to let it be known on the air.

"Good afternoon. I'd like to welcome you to ABC, the network with a heart."

By this time it was common knowledge that John would replace Paar starting October 3, 1962, so his audience took great delight in the darts he threw at ABC.

When pieces of equipment would malfunction, as they so often do on daily shows with little time for rehearsal, he would step back, look at it for a minute, then turn to the audience. "Who invented this, ABC?"

As his time on "Who Do You Trust?" drew to a close, the attacks burst to the surface on the slightest provocation. "Sure ABC's been good to me—$50.00 a week looked awfully good to me back in Omaha!"

He was restless, straining to get on to bigger and better things.

Every night as John tuned in the guest hosts on the "Tonight Show" he almost cried. They were all making shambles of it. NBC had said they would wait for the end of his ABC contract, but that did not stop them from trying every single personality who might have had a remote chance of keeping the "Tonight Show" high in its ratings.

After all, Johnny had a firm twenty-six-week contract. If he did not hack it in that half a year . . . tough!

NBC would use the time spent waiting to conduct on-the-air auditions, just in case the new whiz kid would not be able to hold the audience.

Art Linkletter, Bob Cummings, Merv Griffin, Jack Carter, Jan Murray, Peter Lind Hayes, Soupy Sales, Mort Sahl, Steve Lawrence, Jerry Lewis, Jimmy Dean, Arlene Francis, Jack E. Leonard, Hugh Downs, Groucho Marx, Hal March, and of course Joey Bishop were some of the parade who filed behind the "Tonight Show" desk.

Most, realizing they were just biding time, did just that, yawning their way through program after program. Television sets all across the country began switching off early, not, however, before the sponsors; they started switching off the minute Paar left, promising to come back as soon as Johnny took over—and not a minute before. By the time Carson took over the show, over one-half of the sponsors had cancelled for the summer.

And why not? When Eva Gabor and Jack Carter dancing the Twist is the highlight for an evening, you know the rest of the show is downhill. Al Stevens and his talking dog held the fort one night, but mostly the snores were initiated by shows with guest lists of names nobody recognized, interspersed with home movies of the host.

The Emmy Awards, as well as several other specials, were hosted by Johnny. He filled the rest of his remaining time with his usual schedule of hectic appearances at the Friars' roasts and all the panel shows he had become so familiar to.

By now, the address of Johnny Carson was Sutton Place, Manhattan, and he was living alone. Jody and he had somewhat amiably reached agreement on a divorce. Johnny is still a little fried at Jody's timing. Here he was, about to see the realization of all his dreams and the woman who had stuck with him through thick and thin decides to leave.

After ten years, Jody wanted out.

Johnny Carson is a man who seldom stops working; he never waited around for a big opportunity to fall in his lap and his constant working was a principal cause of the rift.

"My greatest personal failure was when I was divorced from my first wife. That's the lowest I've ever felt—the worst personal experience of my life," he recalls.

It had been pretty rough in Harrison for some time, and the boys were taking the brunt of the beating. "Kids are far better off if there's an honest, clean divorce. I'm happy to notice that my boys don't seem to be negatively affected by mine," John remarked.

So, he moved out of Harrison and onto Sutton Place where he lived alone with occasional visits from tiny, sometime model Joanne Copeland, whom he had met sometime when he was doing the quiz show.

The time of their meeting is hard to determine because

Johnny was still married and neither of them has ever made the date public.

The manner of their meeting was somewhat unique for Joanne, but the circumstances would become all too familiar to the heir-apparent to the "Tonight Show" throne.

Joanne's father had managed to talk Johnny into listening to a tape of his other daughter playing the violin. He arranged to meet Johnny in "Jimmy Comdoms," a local restaurant and bar. When John arrived, he was introduced to Joanne who accompanied her father.

"My Dad introduced us. What could be more old fashioned?" She delights in telling the story, even today after she is no longer married to the man. "When he introduced me, I thought, Johnny Carson? That sounds familiar. Isn't he an announcer or comedian or something?"

After dinner, Johnny and the Copelands sat and listened to the violin tape.

"Well, what do you think of her, Johnny?"

With a deadpan serious face, John looked the proud father straight in the eye. "I think she should quit as soon as possible."

Joanne already knew how well her sister played the violin. "I said to myself, I have to marry this man."

Joanne and Johnny bid goodnight to Dad, and then went out for a couple of drinks. Leaving the last bar, Joanne was aware that something was different. "I suddenly felt everyone staring at me. Well, I knew I was pretty, but I didn't think I was that beautiful." She turned to Johnny at her side. "People are staring at me." He tried to ignore it—better to keep moving and explain it outside. "Is my slip showing or something?" she asked him.

Embarrassed, the color flooding his cheeks, he looked down at her. "I think it's me they're staring at."

That is the first she knew that Johnny was a recognizable figure.

From that point on, the romance bloomed. The fact of his marriage did not seem to bother her because "Johnny's marriage was already on the rocks."

Three weeks was all the time he would have between his

last show on ABC and the first "Tonight Show." John planned to leave Jody and the house in Harrison behind and take producer Art Stark, second banana Ed McMahon, and a lot of hard-earned lessons with him on one of the most incredible rocket rides in show business history—straight to the top, where he now lives.

Chapter Five

To understand the "Tonight Show" and what it had become by the time Carson took over, a brief bit of history would be helpful.

When television first became a viable enterprise capable of earning huge amounts of money for a selected few, it operated under the same rules and guidelines as radio, which was also pouring huge amounts of money into the pockets of the very same selected few people.

Under the system set up by the networks for radio, a manufacturer sponsored a particular show and then underwrote the entire production costs. In turn, only his commercial pitch would be heard. The philosophy of this approach was that people would identify the product with the entertainer and therefore make the connection once again when shopping.

The inference, drawn none too subtly in those early days, was that Arthur Godfrey came your way as a reward for buying Lipton tea. There was the "Colgate Comedy Hour," "Lux Video Theater," and many others, some still with us, like "Hallmark Hall of Fame."

The shows were packaged by advertising agencies and designed primarily to sell their clients' products. The entire show was put together by the agency, who then rented studio space and air time from the networks, making them little more than electronic landlords.

In early 1950 among the myriad ideas and brainstorms to come from the desk of NBC's fanatically prolific president Pat Weaver, was a sales concept for a totally new type of television program. He termed it a magazine format, and the general idea was for the network to produce the shows instead of the agency that was then selling advertising space on the show, much the same way a magazine sells space. In this way, a company unable to afford the tremendous cost of television production could still get their message across to the huge television audiences by buying only a page in Weaver's "magazine," while others bought the rest of the pages, and together they would sponsor the show.

The impetus for this and Weaver's many other NBC projects (among them, "Today," the "Home Show," "Tonight Show," "Your Show of Shows," "Howdy Doody," "Ding Dong School," "Colgate Comedy Hour," "All-Star Review," "Zoo Parade," and "Victory at Sea") was the desire to improve programming. This desire came not so much out of a concern for the American public's best interests, but as a result of RCA's desire to sell more televisions, since they held most of the patents for them. NBC, being owned by RCA, was a logical place to begin giving the public something better to see on their new televisions.

This was RCA's concern and they hired Weaver, who *was* sincerely concerned about the American public's right to know, to do the job.

Born on December 21, 1908 into a middle income family, his father became a millionaire when Pat was in his teens. Immediately upon graduating Dartmouth, Pat left for Paris and the Left Bank, where he unsuccessfully attempted to become a writer. Returning to the United States, he got involved in radio, working his way up the ladder until he was hired by an advertising agency, Young and Rubicam, to produce Fred Allen's "Town Hall Tonight" radio program, eventually going from there to NBC.

Restraint was not a quality found in overabundance around Weaver. Ideas just sort of exploded out of his head, and he sent staff assistants scurrying off to make plans to convert these ideas into realities. His attack against the ad agencies met with great resistance, so he opened up the golden coffers of NBC and out poured money for spectacular sets and the best stars: Benny, Allen, Hope. He paid technicians to experiment with cameras and lighting, all aimed at creating. He did not want a copy of other entertainment forms. He wanted to give television its own place as a creative, immediate art form.

He recorded long interviews with the great thinkers of our time: Bertrand Russell, Robert Frost, Carl Sandburg, Frank Lloyd Wright. He wanted to bring the whole of human experience to the common man while he was sitting in his own living room.

The first attempt at taking the responsibility of production away from the ad agencies started in late night programming, where he felt the resistance would be least. The show was called "Broadway Open House" and it was to star a comedian known as Don "Creech" Hornsby.

The reason the name is so unfamiliar is simply that Don never got to do the show; he died of polio two weeks before the first air date. No one seems to be too positive exactly what it was that Don "Creech" Hornsby did, other than scream "creech, creech, creech" in the middle of a mediocre comedy routine. Someone at NBC must have thought it was hysterically funny.

Filling in on that first attempt at the late night millions were Morey Amsterdam and Jerry Lester who did what was basically an improvisational vaudeville show, complete with all the appropriate leers, raised eyebrows, one-liners, and the rest of the slapstick.

The announcer was Wayne Howell, and the music was supplied by Milton DeLugg on the accordion, backed by four other musicians.

NBC had billed the new offering as a "lighthearted, zany party-type variety show," which it probably would have been if anyone had known what that meant. Lester and Amsterdam did not have the vaguest idea and they proceeded to roll out every old radio gag and vaudeville skit ever dreamt of. It took a bit of scrubbing to get most of it on the air.

The best remembered of the regulars on the show was a young girl by the name of Jennie Lewis. Blonde, reasonably good looking, and with an eye-catching figure, she sat on a stool downstage giving us pearls of wisdom such as "a mushroom is a place where you make love." It did not make much difference; everyone was listening to her figure anyway. She started out as a $75 a week dumb blonde and ended up, when she finally left the show, as a $3,250 a week dumb blonde. In the meantime, they changed her name to Dagmar and she had become the first celebrity created by what was to become the "Tonight Show."

Weaver now had the show and he sent his "magazine" space salesmen into the sticks to sell pages of advertising to the local stations. But the sticks weren't buying. Here was a fresh show every night that was drawing nine out of every ten viewers, but the financial concept was not to the locals' thinking.

NBC offered the show in return for a cut on the commercials the locals ran during the program and the right to run several network commercials also. The local stations said they could keep all the advertising revenue from showing old movies they already owned or could rent for next to nothing, so why should they share with NBC?

NBC reasoned with them. "But we've got nine out of every ten people tuned in and our show is better."

The locals' reasoning went this way. "True. But if none of us carry your show, you won't have *any* viewers."

It is hard to reason with this kind of logic and soon "Broadway Open House" was off the air.

Weaver did not give up, however, and soon he decided to apply his concept to another fringe area of programming no one thought profitable—the early morning hours.

He hired Mort Werner to produce what was to become the "Today Show," patterned along Weaver's "magazine" sales idea. Werner found a lazy voiced, relaxed, easy to live with radio announcer from Chicago named Dave Garroway and finally got the concept off the ground.

Garroway was as easy to live with as any TV personality ever. All across America, TV's started on much the same way radios did when families awoke in the morning. The low-keyed, rambling midwestern easiness of Garroway finally sold Weaver's concept. The locals bought it and loved it. On their own, they had not been able to get anyone to turn a set on in the morning no matter what they did.

Weaver immediately jumped on the issue while it was still hot and got Werner busy on the next "magazine," the "Home Show," which aired in the afternoons. It, too, made it and by mid-1954, he was ready for another attempt at driving the late movies off the set.

In July of that year, Weaver announced that the local affiliates had expressed an eagerness for a major, live, late night television show. The announcement of course was sent to the local affiliates who wanted it just as much as they had wanted "Broadway Open House." The publicity blurb that went out was typical advertising copy: "At a time of night when the 'Great White Way' of Broadway is at its most glamourous, the cameras of 'Tonight' will bring the crossroads of the world to viewers across the country. Acting as Stagedoor Johnny for millions of viewers, 'Tonight' will chat with the stars of Broadway's biggest hits shortly after the curtain drops. Stars and featured entertainers at New York's smartest night clubs will be frequent visitors to the 'Tonight' set."

The blurb went on to tell about the new star of the show, Steve Allen: "He is one of the true native wits to spring into prominence in recent years." The pitch on Steve went on for a whole paragraph, then Weaver's ideas on sales and promotion took up the rest of the pages.

In August, Weaver put together a closed circuit broadcast of the upcoming "Tonight Show" as an added sales boost. Weaver himself appeared, along with Allen, Arlene Francis, and Dave Garroway.

He started the proceedings, announcing "Tonight" as, "The third in NBC's Trinity of Titans!" (The other two being "Today" and "Home.") Then Allen, Francis, and Garroway did plugs and bits, most of which never made it past the censors of 1954, but were funny and apparently did the job, for in September of that year NBC aired the "Tonight Show," offering it to any affiliate who wanted it as far west as Omaha, the end of the transmission lines.

Steve Allen had come to NBC by the somewhat circuitous

73

route of Arizona to Los Angeles to New York, getting his first real acclaim on radio in Los Angeles at radio station KNX, doing basically what the "Tonight Show" now does.

Radio in Los Angeles is as big or bigger than television. Because of the year-round good weather people are loathe to stay inside with the TV, but they take their radios with them.

Steve started out in the Los Angeles area doing a morning comedy show with partner, Wendel Noble, on the Mutual network. After a few shows, they ran out of original material and, afraid to tell the executives, decided to fake it as long as they could, mining old joke books, bad radio scripts, the Sunday comics, anything. They managed to string it out for over five hundred shows.

The next move was to KNX, where he was supposed to do a late night radio program. Steve soon wearied of the format and started turning it into a comedy program as the records got less and less play.

Arriving for work one day, he found a note from the executive offices on his desk: "When we want a comedy show, we'll let you know!"

That night Steve read the memo on the air and asked his listeners to write to the station and "let the executives know" what they wanted. The mail poured in, and eventually Steve convinced the executives that his approach to the program was winning the audience.

From time to time his friends would stop by to watch the program and, as is the case with anyone who specializes in Steve's brand of outrageous humor, spontaneous laughter would be heard in the background. Listeners thought there was a studio audience and started writing in for tickets.

Sensing a good thing, KNX moved him to a bigger studio seating roughly fifty people. Steve was getting big but his salary was not; they kept his pay at the original $100 a week.

The first trip into the audience, now a regular "Tonight Show" feature with both Allen and Carson, came about as a result of a schedule foul-up. Doris Day failed to show up and, left with nothing to fill the gap, Steve grabbed the microphone and headed for what was to turn into his greatest gold mine—the studio audience.

During his days at KNX, Steve managed to get most of the big stars on the show because he had a reputation for not trying to top his guests, something he carried over to the "Tonight Show" and a policy followed for the most part by Carson, if not by Paar.

"Outrageous" is the best word to describe Allen's approach to comedy, or for that matter anything. With Frankie Laine as his guest, he once got into a heated argument over the difficulty of writing songs. Frank maintained that writing songs was a difficult proposition, while Steve insisted that writing them was a cinch, it was getting them published that caused the real aggravation. The argument ended in a wager with Steve betting that he could write fifty songs a day for seven consecutive days. On the air, Frankie bet him $1,000 that he could not do it.

Not only did Allen write the songs on schedule, but he did it in the window of a downtown Los Angeles music store. Of the songs, several were published and two eventually made the charts.

KNX was the same CBS affiliate that started Johnny in Los Angeles, and they seem to have shown the same foresight in placing Steve in good properties. CBS tried Steve everywhere.

Once he replaced Arthur Godfrey and made such an unintentional shambles of the show that everyone thought it was brilliant comedy. Everyone, that is, except the men from the ad agency. They gave him his own show, "The Steve Allen Show," airing it at noon five days a week. The format was what was later refined into the present "Tonight Show." At the same time, Steve was doing a little piece of Saturday-night excitement entitled "Songs For Sale."

Those shows fell by the wayside and two more were cancelled, landing him on "What's My Line?" where Steve had great difficulty recognizing the mystery guests even after he had removed his blindfold.

NBC went out of late night programming in the summer of 1951 with the cancellation of "Broadway Open House;" however, at the same time ABC came on locally with their

own version of a late night variety show hosted by Louis
Nye.

Ted Cott, head of WNBC, the NBC-owned Manhattan station, took one look at the show and thought he could do
better. Ruppert Beer, a locally brewed product, agreed to
sponsor the program and Cott started assembling the necessary people.

He hired the young Dwight Hemion, today one of the best
directors in the business; Gene Rayburn was the announcer;
for a producer he was very lucky when he hired Bill Harbach,
son of the noted composer Otto Harbach.

As was the custom in those days, every show had a resident singer or two. The "Tonight Show" had a young seventeen year old named Steve Lawrence. Soon they added a
young girl to go with Steve. It was Edie Gormet—and she
went with Steve very well.

Allen's ability to work with the odd ball guest was a vital
asset in the early days because no known celebrity would be
seen on the show. Steve had the best odd balls of anyone,
though. The man with the strongest teeth came on and opened beer bottles, which was preferable to the wine expert who
once short-circuited every brain in the Ruppert brewery.

After an intelligent conversation about the merits of wines
from various regions, Steve started to give way to a commercial for their boss, Mr. Ruppert. "I suppose, even though you
are a wine connoisseur, you enjoy a glass of beer every now
and then?"

Without a muscle twitching on his face, the expert replied,
"Beer is for pigs."

Steve wanly smiled and tried to continue. "But this is
Ruppert beer, one of the best brewed, you ought to try
some."

"Beer is for pigs!"

Steve had a woman with the largest wishbone collection in
the world. Once a man with a prize steer came on with the
animal. After Steve and his guest had finished a short bit of
business with the animal, Steve idly inquired, "Where does
this beautiful animal go from here?"

Calmly, the man told Steve, "Straight to the slaughter-house on 14th Street."

The boys in the mailroom got overtime pay for a week after that.

Finally, using his father's influence and name, producer Bill Harbach managed to talk some of the luminaries in the music field to come on the show. After the likes of Richard Rodgers and John Arlen appeared, the rest followed, but the show remained Allen's own personal brand of light insanity.

He tap danced with his fingernails, composed a song from four random notes submitted by the studio audience; he would go into the audience and mine entire shows from the most mundane people to grace a set this side of public service announcements.

The basic reason for the heavy reliance on Steve's talents was the show's budget. Too small to pay celebrity guests their going rate even if the network wanted to, the "Tonight Show" initiated the policy of straight-scale payment to top stars out of necessity. Then it was $240; now, $320.

Steve was the hottest thing in New York, so when Weaver and Werner decided to attack the late movies again they were lucky enough to have the weapon right in their own studio. They merely moved Allen from a local show to a network show.

By now Andy Williams had been added to the singing corps, but NBC wanted them all out.

"Get rid of Steve and Edie," they demanded. "We need bigger names to go network."

Allen was amiable. "Fine. Get me Sinatra and Dinah Shore!" Steve and Edie stayed.

The finances of the show looked something like this: Steve Allen got $3,000 a week to start and soon jumped to $5,000, finally ending with $10,000 a week. The entire "Tonight Show" cost NBC $42,000 a week to produce and they were asking $6,700 a minute for their advertising time.

The show was a success with viewers from the first, but it was a rough uphill battle to sell it to advertisers. After ten months, however, it finally made it over the top and started showing a profit. At times, though, it would fall back into the red, causing NBC once to experiment with shortening the show to one hour, going off the air for a brief period at 12:30 AM.

The reason for the original 11:15 PM starting time, since eliminated by Carson, was Ruppert's insistance that if they were to remain as one of the sponsors, the show would have to continue to start at the same time as it had when Ruppert was the only sponsor. So the show started at 11:15 PM locally and then went on network at 11:30 PM. In the truly insane world of television, this eventually got reversed, the rest of the country getting the show at 11:15 PM and New York not picking it up until 11:30 PM.

The original studio was the old Hudson Theater on West 44th Street. There Steve kept a ladder on which he would sometimes climb into the balcony to do audience interviews.

Allen always loved wild openings and remote pick-ups. The show might start one night with Steve down in the subway interviewing whomever he found, then he might race out of the underground and frantically enter the theater, running through the audience and up onto the stage. Other times he would be lowered in through a window or would sail up into the air dressed as Superman.

Once, though, it got him in trouble. They were in Miami Beach doing a series of shows. Steve looked out his hotel window, high above the "Gold Coast" and all of a sudden it hit him. The most extravagant opening for the "Tonight Show" to date.

At that time, the military was quite willing to use government funds to help film or television crews if there was a little free publicity for them thrown in, so the "Tonight Show" staff contacted the local marine commander, who contacted the local navy admiral, and that night, with tracers flying, flares bursting, and search lights searching, the United States Marines invaded Miami Beach's hotel row.

As the giant steel door of the first landing craft thudded to the sand, Steve walked onto the beach and announced his guests for that night. What he and his staff had neglected to take into consideration was the impending Arab-Israeli war.

78

Thousands of Jewish guests at the finest hotels looked out of their $150 a night windows and became mildly concerned as they watched the mini-armada forming off the coast. Their worst fears were realized as what they thought to be Arabian armies stormed onto the beaches. That night was rough for congressmen and senators from Florida and New York.

Soon the "Tonight Show" became the place to be, and the celebrities flocked to its studios much the same way they continue to do today. Steve is responsible for many television firsts with the "Tonight Show."

He did the first book plug with author Bennett Cerf, who quite prophetically noted the potential impact a television plug might have on book sales.

He did the first single-guest interview. The guest was Carl Sandburg. He did the first one-subject shows with whole nights devoted to drugs, prison reform, civil rights, McCarthyism, and jazz. When he championed the cause of government reform, he had his tires slashed and his life threatened, which is better than the other way around, but disconcerting all the same.

The first sponsor to buy network time on the show was Dr. Land with his then revolutionary Polaroid camera. Steve invested heavily in the new Polaroid stock and it went wild; one of the fringe benefits of doing the show.

Steve was probably the ideal host for the show at that time. Incredibly talented, in addition to his television work he also wrote thousands of songs, twelve books, and several movie scores.

The "Tonight Show" has always created celebrities, but Allen even created some out of the studio audience. He made bona fide names out of Mrs. Sterling who attended every show, as well as Mrs. Miller who still can be seen in the audience of some show every night of the week. He lavished gifts on Mrs. Sterling, but it was never enough, she always asked for more. Mrs. Miller was seen so many times as Steve went up into the audience that AFTRA, the television performers' union, forced her to join.

NBC smelled more lucre and decided to give Allen his own prime time show in addition to the "Tonight Show." The

79

idea was for Steve to draw some of the audience away from Ed Sullivan, which he did with the sometimes absolutely brilliant and always well remembered "Steve Allen Show."

The strain was too much, though, and soon he needed relief, so NBC got Ernie Kovacs to do the "Tonight Show" on Mondays and Tuesdays.

Other changes were taking place higher up at NBC. There had always been bad blood between Weaver and Robert Sarnoff, son of General Sarnoff, thy majority stockholder of the parent company, RCA. Now the war broke out into the open, finally ending with the ousting of Weaver as chairman of the board in 1956. Blood being thicker than talent, there was no other way it could have ended than with NBC firing the only man who saw television as an entity of its own, rather than a copy of someone else's entertainment form. To this day, most of the truly unique elements of television were either first accomplished or proposed by Weaver.

By the end of 1956, Allen had had it with the schedule he was keeping and told NBC that either his Sunday night show went or their "Tonight Show" went. The "Tonight Show," being the ugly duckling it would always remain in the eyes of NBC executives, fell by the boards in late January, 1957.

To replace Allen, NBC came up with a totally different format and changed the name slightly to "Tonight, America After Dark." The idea was for the show to be a little bit of everything: news, gossip, celebrities, remote pickups of fast-breaking news events, light entertainment in the form of the usual acts. It was to be hosted by a group of men in different cities.

In New York the hosts would be columnists Hy Gardner, Bob Considine, and Earl Wilson; in Chicago, Irv Kupcinet, and in Los Angeles it was to be Vernon Scott and Paul Coates. The show's announcer was Jack Lescoulie. All of these involved, save Lescoulie, had absolutely no concept of the medium of television. They brought their newspaper personalities to the show and interviewed guests as if they were writing lurid gossip columns.

Somebody has said they used a lot of wryly captioned,

off-beat photographs on the show, but other than that everyone that appeared was hard to remember, which is a bad sign. No one seems capable of remembering anything anyone ever said or did on the show. The reviews were generous when they said it was the worst idea for a show ever; not only that, the people doing it were so terrible that even if the concept had been good, the whole thing would still stink.

NBC took heed and changed the concept nightly, and nightly the show got worse. With Weaver gone, it became obvious that no one at NBC had the slightest idea about what would work; finally they turned to the then-producer of the "Tonight Show," Dick Linkroum, and told him to "get something on there that will work, or else!"

Linkroum decided to go back to the basic Allen format with another host.

Finding another host was not going to be that easy. NBC, after Allen left, had managed to totally destroy everything in the way of audience and advertisers that Steve had built. Plus, the critics were not going to be so kind as to compare the new host with the ineptness of "Tonight, America After Dark," but instead would compare him to Allen and Kovacs.

After sounding out every unemployed actor, announcer, and celebrity, Linkroum approached Jack Paar.

Starting in radio, Paar had made a good name for himself during the war as a special services entertainer, spending most of his time in trouble having bitterly attacked the officer corps from the stage.

Paar moved into television shortly after the war and was always available to fill the gap on a substitute basis; in short, he was Joey Bishop before Joey Bishop became Joey Bishop.

For a while he had a morning show on CBS which was very well received and eventually began to draw some of Garroway's audience. But mostly, Paar was known as an amiable, personable performer available to fill in where needed.

Linkroum had a hunch that Paar might be able to pull it off; besides, there was no one else of any caliber who was interested. He approached him and Jack practically went down on his knees begging for the job.

Linkroum gave him the OK and Paar said, "That Linkroum, he's great, he's a genius. I'll always be eternally grateful to him.

Within six months Paar had Linkroom barred from the set of the "Tonight Show" and shortly thereafter, Linkroum was handed his pink slip and showed the door; but Jack was eternally thankful to him for those six months.

In September of 1957, Paar officially took over as new host. The problems he faced seemed monumental. There was no other word for what he was taking over; it was an unqualified bomb. The indifference of the advertisers was matched only by the audience attitude. The show had clearance problems and better and better films were now being sold to television.

NBC gave him skimpy sets and lighting, which made the show look as if it were being shot in the year 1857. The cameramen had difficulty keeping Jack in the camera lens frame while he was seated at his desk; when he got up to do bits, it looked as if the cameras were being hand-held. The odds were long. In many quarters there was no betting on the show, as most everybody assumed that Paar would not be able to pull it off.

Jack got an old army buddy, José Melis, to lead the orchestra and managed to latch onto one of the better, more articulate announcers in Hugh Downs.

The general opinion at that time was much the same as when Carson replaced Paar. "What can he possibly do to follow Allen and Kovacs?"

Jack had been around the industry, experiencing his fair share of success and failure (more of the latter than the former) and waxed philosophically at the pessimists. "They can't put a knife in my back because there's no room. It's all broken blades!"

"America After Dark" had a rating of 135 out of 135 shows rated. Paar tried anything to improve it. He had the slightly bizzare Jack Douglas, a writer who had been with him for over ten years, on the show doing some of his outrageous bits in an effort to recapture parts of the Allen audience. He brought on Peter Ustinov to tell his stories. The numbers started to climb. Then there was Dody Goodman, Elsa Maxwell, and Hermione Gingold. The audience was coming back. Jack liked the new numbers and so did NBC.

If Allen could get shows out of the audience, so could he, and Jack headed for the general public. Except it did not work—he was petrified of them. Once in an effort to embarrass Mrs. Sterling, the sweet old lady Steve had lavished so many gifts on, he asked her to stand up and then said, "I suppose the reason you're here is to get more gifts."

"No," Mrs. Sterling answered, "I come here because I'm lonely."

Jack retreated to the stage and seldom went back. An associate of that time summed up Jack's fear of the people out there by saying, "He doesn't even like someone else's shadow to fall on him."

He discovered Jonathan Winters and Genevieve, a pert, blonde actress who had tremendous problems with the English language. She became "undiscovered" when Jack left the air. The future was looking up, but some critics who still hungered for Allen wrote, "The 'Tonight Show' consists of people sitting around trying to change the subject."

Then Jack discovered that he could turn the one thing he did naturally, and did better than anyone else, into ratings and success—aggravate people, create controversy, act as the match to a drum of gasoline spilled onstage.

He had never found difficulty in finding trouble, starting with his first radio job, which he landed by forcing himself on a radio announcer doing man-in-the-street interviews in Jackson, Michigan, where the family had moved from Canton, Ohio, Jack's birthplace. The radio station heard the interview and hired him at $3.00 a week for part-time work.

At eighteen he left home and knocked around the country from radio station to radio station. Somewhere along the way, he managed to marry the same girl twice. Now that's trouble!

Inducted in 1942, he went into special services and earned a good reputation, mostly from an article in *Esquire* magazine about the men entertaining the troops, ". . . doing a job that had to be done. Making men laugh in the most laugh-proof places in the world."

While on stage in Okinawa, he noticed a navy commodore come in late with one of the better looking nurses and decided to give the audience, predominately enlisted men, a good laugh. "We were going to have six lovely girls do the dance of the virgins, but they broke their contracts by being with the commodore," he quipped. All eyes turned to the couple trying to find a seat. "You'd think one man and a broad wouldn't hold up five thousand enlisted men!" he added.

At the end of the show Paar walked off stage to be greeted by a navy shore patrol detachment. They arrested him and served him with court marshal papers. The army intervened and managed to bail him out by promising that they would have him off Okinawa within hours of his release.

The *Esquire* article got him a one-shot contract with RKO pictures, where he appeared opposite Marilyn Monroe in the best-forgotten "Love Nest." Jack went back to radio.

With good reviews from a stint as the summer replacement for Jack Benny, Jack landed his own show on ABC, where his talent for the indiscreet remark cut his stay there to three months. He attacked everybody.

Going from there to substituting, with several shows of his own thrown in along the way, "Bank On The Stars" and "Up To Paar" preceded his replacement of Walter Cronkite on the CBS "Morning Show," and then, on to the "Tonight Show."

Elsa Maxwell, the globular member of the Paar Television Family, usually attacked everyone anyway, so when she mentioned columnist Walter Winchell, no one thought anything of it. Jack continued the conversation by noting that he thought Winchell was "out to get him." That was all Elsa needed. She launched into a tirade against the columnist, that coming from another source might have been grounds for slander.

Winchell, never one to turn his back after the gauntlet had been thrown, took up the challenge in his column, and day after day the venom oozed from the paper and the television screen. Charges and counter-charges were hurled, with Elsa accusing Winchell of never voting. Winchell countered with a picture of him leaving a voting booth, which Paar looked at and pooh-poohed.

Winchell went to the courts and sued, not the "Tonight Show," but their advertisers, for $2,000,000, claiming that the slander of his name on the show had resulted in that loss to the Damon Runyon Cancer Research Fund, which he was associated with.

Winchell was the last of the tyrannical powers in the newspaper business. There was almost no one he could not squeeze where it hurt, and he had no compunctions about doing it. He squeezed NBC and Elsa was gone—end of controversy.

But it was just the beginning for Jack. When critics would hint at his not being the equal of Allen, he accused Steve of stealing material from him. "Furthermore, Steve Allen is just plain unfunny," he countered.

The ratings zoomed. He was the talk of practically every gathering. Here was something new; no one knew what would happen at 11:30 PM, but more often than not, sparks would fly as Jack picked fights with everyone: Ed Sullivan, the U.S. Senate, Jimmy Hoffa, Dorothy Kilgallen, the newspapers, CBS Chairman of the Board William Paley, and everyone who worked for him.

Like him or not, Jack did not hold much back; he gushed all over our living rooms and bedrooms. He got angry, irate, happy, mad, sad, elated, surprised. He laughed, cried, and hurt for us.

A regular feature on the "Tonight Show" during Paar's tenure was the confession. Jack would get himself caught in what would look to us like the most embarrassing situation; and then, just at the moment we all expected the egg to run down his face and onto the desk, Jack would confess all, throwing himself on our mercy. It worked for him time and time and time again.

The first time it worked for him was when he "discovered" a new singer, Trish Dwelly. She appeared on the show the same day she ostensibly auditioned, wearing the same clothes, a sweater and skirt, she had worn to the audition. There was no time for her to change. She sang several numbers and the press went wild.

"A star is born!" In the truest Hollywood tradition, Jack had "discovered" another giant talent. She was offered record contracts, screen tests, and Paar signed her on as a full-fledged member of the Tonight Family.

It wasn't long before someone realized that it just does not happen that way and started nosing around. Soon it was discovered that Trish was a professional singer who had sung with several groups and appeared on other television shows, the "Perry Como Show" among them.

Fraud!

Jack came on and apologized for being "naive." Neither he, nor his staff had bothered to ask Trish if she had had any professional experience, so she hadn't really lied to them.

Anytime you want to be on the "Tonight Show," you just go over to Rockefeller Center and tell the casting people there that you don't have any professional experience but you would like to be on the show and see how fast you get in front of the cameras.

Jack stood there and took the heat. "OK, I'm naive. I thought I had made a discovery. Well, I still think I have made a discovery!"

Within two weeks she was gone. The official reason given was that her costumes and arrangements were too expensive. The country, by now, had gone Paar mad. There were now five million people who tuned in every night. Everyone was all "one big happy family." Jack included us in his family life, showing films of his wife Miriam and his beloved daughter Randy. When Jack had trouble with the commuter traffic, we all had trouble. If Randy sneezed, we all wiped our noses.

The "Tonight Show" was now being bought by 115 stations coast to coast, and the advertising revenues were climbing well past $10,000,000 annually. Jack's salary was $2,750 a week.

The Tonight Family ebbed and flowed as members came and went with Jack's whims. Gone were Dody Goodman and a sexy weather lady named Tedi Thurman. Bil and Cora Baird with their amazing puppets lasted a little while and then they exited to be replaced by Reiko, Jack Douglas' kooky Japanese wife, Zsa Zsa, who came and did her thing, and Hermione, who was still around. Pat Harrington, who would later reach a form of mini-fame as one of Steve Allen's men in the street, became a regular, as did Hans Conried with his sophisticated show business stories. Peggy Cass and Mary Margaret McBride talked with the likes of Alexander King or laughed at the barbed tongue of Oscar Levant.

Levant's stories and observations were the best. Always slightly acid, they never left any doubt about Oscar's feelings. They became some of the most quoted of television quotes, for example, "Elizabeth Taylor should get the 'other woman of the year' award." Levant's observations that ballet is the fairy's baseball game, and that a newsreel is a series of catastrophies ending in a fashion show were always well received.

It was not all talk; at times Jack would have the entertainers on to do their bits, the best of which were the incomparable Mike Nichols and Elaine May routines and of course the slightly perverse comical genius of Jonathan Winters.

New careers were launched by Jack from what appeared to be nothing more than a mildly amusing late night filler. He started doing a segment of the show entitled "What ever happened to?" during which he brought on people who had enjoyed some amount of notoriety in their lives but were now forgotten. The most successful resurrection of this type was Cliff Arquette, who was a regular on the old "Fibber Magee and Molly" radio program. His appearances on the "Tonight Show" started him on an entirely new career. He landed his own show on ABC, but that folded when he got away from his basic Charley Weaver character that the public seemed so in tune with. Arquette wrote a best selling book and was considered an authority on the American Civil War. But it was game shows where he made his mark, and it is from there that most of us are likely to remember the puckish, dirty old man known as Charley Weaver.

Arquette brought one other thing to the attention of late night America: "Hurley's." Among the stone monoliths of Rockefeller Center there stands on the corner of 49th Street and Sixth Avenue a testament to perseverance and individuality known as *Hurley's*. It is a bar, and at the time the Rockefellers were amassing the land on which to build their center, Hurley's held out for more money. The offers from the Rockefellers went up and up, but the owners of the building held out. Finally, John D. Rockefeller gave up and built his "city within a city" around the site, leaving the Victorian tenement housing Hurley's standing like a pimple on John Davidson's face.

Arquette talked incessantly about Hurley's because he spent a good deal of his life there, as did Ed McMahon when he took up residence on the "Tonight Show" couch. Hurley's still stands in its familiar spot, and a stray celebrity calming his nerves before an evening broadcast can be found frequenting the premises.

Allen had received some static concerning the number and frequency of commercials on the "Tonight Show," but as Paar attracted a bigger and bigger audience, the show increasingly sold out. To a public used to the relatively limited number of commercials on prime time television, the plugs seemed never ending, and they always came in the middle of something interesting. For Allen it was not that much of a problem to pick up where he had left off but for Paar, who relied so heavily on the proper mixture of guests to achieve friction, and eventually fire, through debate, the commercials became something more than a nuisance. It fostered studies and surveys and endless newspaper and magazine pieces, as well as food for even more frothing conversation on the show. The gripes and defenses aired on the show drew yet more criticism from the advertisers, who did not want a discussion of the merits of commercials in any form.

All the yapping and yelling, the desk thumping and complaining meant only one thing: more and more Americans were getting less sleep as increasing numbers stayed up to see what was going to happen next.

By 1958 Paar's success translated into 115 stations carrying the show, which rang the NBC cash registers up to almost $15 million a year in advertising revenues. For his part, Jack was getting, in addition to his $2,750.00 a week salary, a cut on most of the commercials, a six-week vacation, and Mondays and Fridays off. Taped reruns were showed on Fridays.

During the time of the Paar "Tonight Show" rumors of discord always slipped from NBC. As Jack began looking at the audience he was generating for NBC, he became more secure in his place behind the desk, and with that the discord began to boil to the surface. Jack Paar can certainly read a newspaper, but he was probably the last person to realize his own impact on the American public. When he finally did realize it, he flexed his muscles and became the most controversial and probably the most disliked man at NBC. He began cancelling guests because of personal likes and dislikes. No one seemed capable, in his eyes, of attaining the high artistic plane demanded by him. Jack was forever on the air complaining about the "hacks and incompetents" surrounding him.

For a man who overcame a childhood speech impediment by talking with a mouth full of buttons (he had gotten the idea from the Greek legend of Demosthenes, who is said to have done the same thing except with pebbles), he had come a long way. And he had a long way yet to go. The real controversy, the *big* rows were still to come.

His concern for the plight of the Cuban people led him to do whole shows on that beleaguered island. His program attempted to show both sides of the question, giving us a look at Batista and his followers. We saw the way they lived, the lush Caribbean opulence of those who were born into the right families, or who were willing to live Batista's lies while ignoring the squalor most of their countrymen were forced to endure. Then Jack gave us a look at Fidel and his promises of a new and better lot for the Cuban people. As the American public looked at the horror of Batista's political prisons, Jack left us with the implication that all of the horrors and inequities would disappear under Castro's hand. With the benefit of hindsight, we can see today Jack's naiveté in showing us two sides of a counterfeit coin, but in those days Paar believed it when Fidel told him of the high moral purpose of the revolution.

Any program that has the potential for the unexpected, as

the "Tonight Show" does, is going to have its share of problems and difficulties in the dilemma of giving equal time to conflicting views. Jack created an art form with the problem by allowing the guest to plug the wrong thing in the first place; then when the executives complained, he would mention these complaints and reopen the issue. At long last when the entire problem was ironed out, Jack usually would make mention of it one more time, with an appropriate comment and apology thrown in, just to keep all the NBC executives happy. But Jack got into trouble for giving improper plugs to stocks and real estate companies as well as many others.

A man equally capable of creating controversy was Robert F. Kennedy. He made his first appearance on the "Tonight Show" while he was Chief Counsel for the Labor Investigating Select Senate Committee on Improper Activities in Labor or Management Fields. It was the beginning of a love affair between Jack and the Kennedy family. Bobby came on to talk about unsavory characters worming their way into organized labor. With Paar's urging, and assuring that Bobby could say anything he wanted, the future Attorney General launched his first public attack on teamster boss Jimmy Hoffa. Kennedy warned the American public of the danger of letting "people like this" take the management of organized labor away from the honest workers. The appearance created quite a stir, both pro and con.

Never one to keep his feelings bottled up for too long, on one occasion Paar found talking to Mickey Rooney an impossibility. Rooney was stone drunk and was making a shambles of the show. After several attempts at being tactful, Jack mentioned that he didn't think coming on the show drunk was professional behavior for an actor of his stature.

Rooney replied, "Listen, I'm no fan of yours. I don't care to watch your show!"

Stung, Jack merely said, "Would you care to leave?"

Mickey left, but later when he showed up at Jack's hotel with several of the gorillas he was known to travel with, Jack showed a measure of discretion untypical of him, and made amends with Mickey.

What Jack knew about sensation and controversy and how to use them to manipulate the public Dorothy Kilgallen had forgotten before the invention of television. She had been trying sensationalism to pump newspaper sales for years and saw the perfect foil in Paar. She started by attacking him for his pro-Castro stand and went on to call him the ultimate 50s dirty word: "Communist!" Jack countered by pointing out her inadequacies as a journalist. He criticized her for the manner in which she covered stories and finally, when both of them had just about run out of steam, Jack got around to commenting on her lack of a chin. In the long run, their bickering amounted to a great big nothing, except that additional hundreds of thousands of people had tuned in the show or bought newspapers to read about this particular bit of nothing.

There were not many secrets Jack kept from his public. He did not go out much; he commuted between his wife Miriam and his daughter Randy in their Bronxville house and the studio; he hated parties; and basically he seemed to be a pretty straight-laced family man. He would occasionally wander into the risqué side of the spectrum with a slightly off-color story from time to time, but it was never anything anyone would be shocked at hearing from a minister today. Jack had always been careful of sexually-oriented stories; that is why NBC's decision to edit the now famous "W.C." story seemed so bizarre. To Jack, bathroom stories apparently did not count as risqué—and one night he told what he considered a "cute" bathroom story. He watched the tape of the show that night and found that the story had been deleted. It had been cut without his knowledge.

For weeks before, the pressure had been building to the point where one of his staff remarked, "Jesus, is he strung out these days. Something's going to blow."

It was Jack who blew, right up out of his seat behind the desk and out the door of the studio.

A headline in a West Coast newspaper shouted, "PAAR FIRES NETWORK!"

The following night Jack came on and proceeded to run a

normal "Tonight Show" for the first twenty minutes. He then began talking about his difficulties with NBC, explaining that they had cut a cute story he had told the night before. He resented being treated like a little boy who needed his fingers slapped. After a sleepless night agonizing over the proper course of action, he said: "I've made a decision about what I'm going to do. And only one person knows about this—it's Hugh Downs. My wife doesn't know about it, but I'll be home in time and I'll tell her." The show was taped earlier in the day and he would be able to get to Bronxville before airtime. "I'm leaving the 'Tonight Show'," he announced.

All across the country those watching called friends, "Turn on the 'Tonight Show.' Paar just quit!" No one was leaving the set for midnight snacks or bathroom calls; Jack had their undivided attention.

"I took over a show with sixty stations, there are now 158; this show is sold out; it's the highest, I think, producer for this network, and I believe I was let down by this network at a time when I could have used their help."

He told the audience that they'd always been great to him, turned, shook hands with Hugh Downs, and walked quietly out of the studio.

Downs ran the rest of the show from his seat on the couch, choosing to leave Jack's chair empty for the rest of the night. Downs, who had always brought a measure of reason to Jack's outbursts, quietly told the audience, "Jack frequently does things he regrets. But I'd like to think this is not final and that he will be back."

Hugh and the two guests for that night, Shelley Berman and Orson Bean, sat around discussing Jack's departure for the rest of the show, for the most part agreeing with Jack's position.

What follows is the entire W.C. story Jack told. The reason for its inclusion is not only to shed some light on Jack's problems with the network, but also to point out the great distances we have traveled in the way of acceptability of TV material.

An English lady, while visiting in Switzerland, was looking for a room, and she asked the schoolmaster if he could recommend any to her. He took her to see several rooms, and when everything was settled, the lady returned to her home to make the final preparations to move. When she arrived home, the thought suddenly occurred to her that she had not seen a W.C. (Water Closet) around the place. So she immediately wrote a note to the schoolmaster asking him if there was a W.C. around. The schoolmaster was a very poor student of English, so he asked a parish priest if he could help in the matter. Together they tried to discover the meaning of the letters W.C., and the only solution they could find for the letters was a Wayside Chapel. The schoolmaster then wrote to the English lady the following note:

Dear Madam:

I take great pleasure in informing you that the W.C. is situated nine miles from the house you occupy, in the center of a beautiful grove of pine trees surrounded by lovely grounds.

It is capable of holding 229 people and it is open on Sunday and Thursday only. As there are a great number of people and they are expected during the summer months, I would suggest that you come early: although there is plenty of standing room as a rule.

You will no doubt be glad to hear that a good number of people bring their lunch and make a day of it, while others who can afford to go by car arrive just in time. I would especially recommend that your ladyship go on Thursday when there is a musical accompaniment.

It may interest you to know that my daughter was married in the W.C. and it was there that she met her husband. I can remember the rush there was for seats. There were ten people to a seat ordinarily occupied by one. It was wonderful to see the expression on their faces.

The newest attraction is a bell donated by a wealthy

resident of the district. It rings every time a person enters. A bazaar is to be held to provide plush seats for all the people, since they feel it is a long-felt need. My wife is rather delicate, so she can't attend regularly.

I shall be delighted to reserve the best seat for you if you wish, where you will be seen by all. For the children, there is a special time and place so that they will not disturb the elders. Hoping to have been of service to you, I remain,

Sincerely,
The Schoolmaster

For days the story of Paar quitting was a major news item. At NBC, where Jack was never personally that popular, the feelings were mixed. Many were openly thankful that he was gone while others recognized his popularity with the audience and, with an eye to the yearly income statements, regretted his leaving.

The phones rang non-stop at NBC, where extra clerical help had been hired to handle the tons of mail pouring into the studio. The agents were on the wires too, with promises that their clients could easily fill Jack's shoes, but the big brass knew better. "Promise him anything, but get him back!"

Jack had left for Hong Kong and didn't appreciate the full impact of his absence. Because he had made a fair number of enemies, not all the reports bemoaned his leaving. But others knew full well that Paar had been the only person to step on sacred cows on the air, and they begged him to return.

Jack Gould of the *New York Times* wrote: "Mr. Paar is not the traditional trouper; he is a creation of television. If he began as a light humorist, his forte on his own show has been an outspokeness that has not alienated viewers weary of nice nellyism and self-appointed sacred cows who can dish out criticism but cannot take it."

On the other side John Crosby wrote a piece entitled, "The Fall of Jack Paar," in which he said Jack was washed up and, even if he wanted it, he couldn't have his old job back.

Five weeks later Jack was back. "When I walked off, I said there must be a better way of making a living. Well, I've looked, and there isn't. Be it ever so humble, there is no place like Radio City." He went on to apologize for his childish behavior, but he said, "I'm totally unable to hide what I feel." He went on to serve fair warning to NBC that they might expect similar action in the future if he were pushed to it. He also said that he intended to continue to throw snowballs with rocks in them, and then, just so everyone would know he was back, he launched into another attack of Walter Winchell, who hadn't been particularly kind to Jack during his absence.

Later, when he was in a mellow concilitory mood, he allowed NBC to chop several minutes out of the show to avoid still more lawsuits from Winchell's lawyers. By this time both NBC and Paar realized that Jack Paar was a man who would always be in trouble of some kind, and that trouble meant viewers. So, the network began to loosen up on Jack, giving him more of a free hand. Now, instead of allowing controversy to find him, Jack went out and searched for it. Seldom did he miss finding it.

Soon after his return, he brought John F. Kennedy, then a presidential aspirant, on the show and allowed him to go through his pitches. Many said that his appearance was instrumental in his later nomination as the Democratic party's candidate for the 1960 elections. Later Paar had the Nixons, Pat and Dick, on the show, during which they asked for Paar's autograph for their two daughters, Tricia and Julie. Despite his fawning and constant currying favor with the Kennedy clan, Paar's politics became increasingly pro Nixon.

Soon another feud was in the works as Ed Sullivan refused to pay any performers who appeared on the Paar show more than the same $320.00 they received from Paar. Jack accused Sullivan of depriving entertainers of a living wage and devoted several shows to scathing broadsides aimed at him. Paar then tore into the press for their preferential treatment of Sullivan. He invited Ed onto the "Tonight Show" to talk their differences out. Sullivan accepted and then failed to show up on the day appointed. On that day, Hugh Downs ran the show for the first fifteen minutes and then introduced Jack as a guest. Jack came out and delivered a one-hour diatribe against Sullivan. He claimed that Ed had first suggested that he come on the show and read a prepared text from a telepromter rather than debate the point.

To this Paar added, "Any idiot can read a Teleprompter!"

Then, almost as an afterthought, he said, "Ed Sullivan is a liar. That is libel. He must now sue and go to court. Under oath, I repeat, Ed Sullivan, you lied today."

Sullivan saw that there was no way of him ever coming out on top and dropped the entire matter, but in traditional Paar style, the matter was not yet closed.

Weeks after the original tempest boiled over, Jack Benny, one of the few truly good human beings in a business re-knowned for barracudas, called Paar to task while a guest on the "Tonight Show." Paar had asked Benny to play the violin and Benny replied, "I'll play if you let me say something to you, and promise that you won't get angry. You've got to promise."

Paar promised and Benny told him that sometimes he thought Paar was absolutely nuts. He went on to explain that Sullivan was one of his dearest friends and that he had not called Paar any names, despite Paar's slanders of Sullivan. Then he said, "Now, with all the trouble there is in the world today, why should you and he have fights? I mean, if you're going to be mad at someone be mad at Eichman or some-body." Benny went on to say that he knew Jack did not mean any of the things he had said about Sullivan. Then he asked Jack to apologize, "Now, you tell everybody you're sorry. Now say it. Say you're sorry."

With a big emotional gush, out it came. "I'm sorry! I'm sorry!"

With the apology, or confession, the cycle was complete and Paar was free to move on to the next storm—to the south in Cuba. The abortive Bay of Pigs invasion was still in the news when Jack came upon an idea for releasing the prisoners held by his friend, Castro. He would trade tractors, which

Jack thought were desperately needed in Cuba, for the prisoners. When Fidel didn't even bother to respond to Paar's offer, the entire episode was quickly forgotten.

In response to the Communist partition of Berlin, Paar decided to take the "Tonight Show" to Germany and give the late night public a first-hand look at tyranny in action. He took his family as well as Peggy Cass.

Jack went to within fifteen feet of the dividing line between east and west at the Friedrichstrasse gate, the only opening in the wall not sealed to traffic. He conducted interviews with soldiers and saw a demonstration of the army's new M-14 rifle.

As in previous situations, the military had a difficult time staying away from free publicity, and this was not to be an exception. They moved extra troops up to the wall along with anti-tank guns and machine guns, and made sure they all got on camera. Paar closed the show by explaining that he was not there as a journalist, but more as a social commentator. He went on in closing, ". . . but we tried to bring you the story of what is happening here."

The story got through loud and clear. The press attacked Paar for using the military to boost his show. They jumped on him for foolishly meddling in areas where delicate negotiations were in progress. Some even went so far as to say that he had nearly turned the cold war into a hot one.

To explain why the greatest show of military might seen in Berlin since the dispute started there, Jack said they had come to see him because, "I am the best show in town."

He was the best show in many towns, Washington among them. In the United States Senate several legislators demanded that Paar be investigated, that at the very least, he come to Washington and explain his conduct, to which Jack quipped, "It's going to get a hell of a rating for the show."

A week after the Berlin Wall incident Jack was off to Russia, where he traveled as a tourist, managing to get back to the United States without further incident. Once in America, Jack retaliated by attacking those who had attacked him in the press and in Washington. Rightfully so, he pointed out that all the fuss and criticism had taken place before the Berlin show was aired. The entire furor was created out of exaggerated news reports and rumors.

In speaking of the press he said, "Some members of the Fourth Estate act like members of the Fourth Reich." He then went on the offensive attacking Jack Gould, members of the United States Senate, Dorothy Kilgallen, Lee Mortimer, *Life, Newsweek*, The *New York Journal American*, The *Chicago Sun Times*, The *Chicago Tribune* and Irv Kupcinet. Never let it be said that Jack Paar was prone to half measures.

When he finally got around to Irv Kupcinet, he called attention to something unpleasant that had happened to Kup some years before. With that attack, Jack Paar got a bit of his own medicine.

The attack did not come from the outside where Jack might have expected it. It came from the couch to his right. Hugh Downs was incensed. "I don't think what you did in Berlin was wrong, but I think part of what you did tonight was wrong." Paar was suitably meek as he realized Downs meant business: ". . . to attack on a basis that you did a guy like Kupcinet, who is a friend of mine, I think is off base. . . . When you attack injustice, when you attack principles that are wrong, you do so more effectively by not putting it on a personal basis. That's what grieves me. . . . You don't need it!"

Year after year one emotional deluge followed by another finally took its toll. Paar was drawn to a thin wire that responded to every touch. He whined and moaned, erupted at the slightest touch, but soon realized that he could be drawn no tighter. Shortly after returning from Europe he told NBC that he was quitting the "Tonight Show" for good. He would remain until March 30, 1962; by then NBC would have to have someone else to sit behind the desk.

NBC responded by offering him a new five-year contract with more than double his present salary. When that did not work, they even went as far as to offer him ownership of the show. Still no go; Jack was leaving. The main reason was the tension and exhaustion as he had already explained, but never losing a beat, Jack also said one of his reasons for leaving the show was the increasing censorship he found in television. He could not find freedom of speech any more.

"If you don't believe me, let any union member, any little guy in a union, get up and say a few unpleasant truths about the big shots who run it. He'll see how far freedom of speech gets him; or try sometime at the next PTA meeting." Not only that, he also said there should be more controversy and debates; there should be more curiosity and questions in our country.

On March 29 the last "Tonight Show" opened with Jack E. Leonard introducing celebrities who had dropped in to say goodbye. It took him a full fifteen minutes just to read the names. José Melis played a medley of music used on the show and then at 11:30 Jack Paar came onto the stage of the "Tonight Show" for the last time as the regular host. He received a standing ovation that seemed interminable. It was the end of 24,000 hours of programming. They showed film clips of products that had not worked and moments that had. There were film sequences of people who had been on the show saying goodbye to Jack; Bobby Kennedy, Billy Graham, and Tallulah Bankhead among them.

Robert Merrill, of the Metropolitan Opera, closed out the show singing "Pagliacci." Jack said his goodbyes and then, with tears streaming down his face, he turned and walked from the stage.

The familiar "Tonight" slide came on, except this time it said, "NO MORE TO COME."

There was indeed no more to come. The last Paar "Tonight Show" has brought down the curtain on a type of television programming not to be seen again. From now on the audience would know what to expect of a television program; no more surprises. Gone were the electric sparks, the tears, the outrage, the pettiness, and childish pique. There would be no one to make a rash error and then come on the air and apologize. Guests would no longer become so enraged in debate that they would stand, square off, and threaten to punch the other in the mouth.

Paar attempted, almost ten years later, to come back to late night programming, but it did not work. In fact, his late night return on ABC proved to be embarrassingly bad. We no longer knew Jack and therefore no longer cared. We had no investment any more in Miriam and Randy; most of the old hobgoblins were either retired or dead; and with today's pressures for instant success, there was no time to get to know Jack all over again. He was never an entertainer with slick routines or a glib manner that could cover—all prerequisites of an American public fed a television diet of nothing else during Paar's absence.

The newsmen who formerly had printed nothing but the dull releases handed out by the hacks in Washington, began to question. They were goaded by an involved, hip, younger generation, and they diminished our desire for controversy, cured us of a need for bombast and excitement, and took Jack Paar's place on television.

Chapter Six

Mort Werner had hired Steve Allen and Jack Paar. He was now about to hire Johnny Carson, proclaiming that the three were identical. When pressed later for an explanation of that statement he said: "Allen, Paar, and Carson have one thing in common: they have all done everything that can be done on broadcasting. They don't need prepared material or rehearsals. . . . The "Tonight Show" is the open forum of the entertainment world, which makes it tough to control and it also has a unique and complicated business construction. The man who is running it has to know, first and foremost, how to drive the train. He has to know when to stop for commercials, where to go when he starts up again, and how to keep the train on the track. . . . All we ask is that he devote his whole life to the program."

In Carson, Werner had made the right choice. Unlike Steve Allen, whose incredible array of interests kept him constantly jumping from one project to another, or Paar who never seemed quite sure that TV was to be his lifetime career, Carson, in time, became positive that this was where he wanted to be. In the time since he has taken over the show, he has so indelibly marked late night programming that it might be impossible to change it even after he leaves.

The six months until October 3, Carson's first night on the "Tonight Show," seemed endless to Johnny. Not only did he have to continue his daily routine on "Who Do You Trust?," but now he had to begin a press campaign aimed at familiarizing the television public who did not watch daytime TV with his name. Reporters from every conceivable publication descended on him. For a while, Johnny thought New York was inhabited by nothing but press people.

At one point, he got so tired of the constant prying and questioning, all to find out who was this skinny young man about to replace Paar, that he issued a set of answers to prospective interviews.

1. Yes I did.
2. Not a bit of truth in that rumor.
3. Only twice in my life, both times on Saturday.
4. I can do either, but I prefer the first.
5. No. Kumquats.
6. I can't answer that question.
7. Toads and tarantulas.
8. Turkestan, Denmark, Chile, and the Komandorskie Islands.
9. As often as possible, but I'm not very good at it yet. I need much more practice.
10. It happened to some old friends of mine and it's a story I'll never forget.

A funny bit, but successive legions of reporters were to find during those first few months on the "Tonight Show," that those ten answers were all Johnny Carson was going to divulge about himself. The show he would be more than happy to talk about, but his personal life, unlike Paar's, was to be Johnny's concern and not the press's, and that is still the case today.

Single again, this period found Johnny out on the town more often than ever before. With him as a drinking buddy, was his second banana on "Who Do You Trust?" Ed McMahon, a man who knew more about drinking buddies and going out on the town than W.C. Fields himself. Both men were regulars on the night circuit, and neither felt any pain as a rule. Without a family to go home to, the club hopping provided some form of a relief from the pressures building on Johnny. Not only was he following one of the most successful acts in television, he was being asked to take over the highest money maker on TV.

Johnny announced that he would keep the basic format of desk and couch used partially by Allen and exclusively by Paar, but, as he kept pointed out in interview after interview, "I am not going to try and imitate Paar."

Johnny stressed that, rather than controversy, he was going to aim exclusively at entertainment. His job, as he saw it, was to be amusing. He also pointed out that all humor is at someone's expense, and toes were bound to be stepped on. For example, one time as a guest on the "Steve Allen Show" he mentioned a newspaper item concerning the theft of mobster Mickey Cohen's car. Cohen's dog was in the car and was stolen too. Johnny telling the story finished with, ". . . I understand the police haven't found the car yet, but they caught the dog holding up a liquor store." The next day his telephone was ringing and on the other end was a Runyonesque voice, warning of the consequences of poking fun at Mickey.

Johnny protested, "It wasn't Mickey I was talking about. It was the dog!"

"Mickey don't care. Just don't do it no more," was the reply.

The warning must have worked because Johnny stopped telling jokes about Mickey Cohen's dog. Johnny went on to explain that there will always be a lunatic fringe who will call to complain about anything you do on the air. It became obvious, however, that John had no intention of stepping on the vast number of toes Paar had. As one NBC executive put it, "Paar brought us an anxiety neurosis. Carson brings us a tranquilizer."

Spontaneity was one quality Johnny was shooting for; he said there would be little or no rehearsal for the show. Nice press, but it seemed highly unlikely that the "Tonight Show" would be the first place Johnny Carson would choose to go on unprepared and unrehearsed, especially since some of his competition in certain local markets would be Steve Allen. Johnny would be prepared. He described his job this way, "The 'Tonight Show' job is mainly to be a catalyst. Keep things moving. You have to quickly sense dull moments and change your gait."

The "Tonight Show" desk was not unfamiliar to Johnny. He had subbed for one night all the way back in 1958, eventually working his way up from a couple of days to filling in for two weeks during Paar's vacation. Paar himself had gone as far as to say on the air that Johnny was the man to replace him. Johnny responded by saying that he admired Paar. Things were not to stay that amiable for long.

The salary NBC was to pay John came out to a little over $100,000 a year on a five-year contract. The show, at the time Carson took it over, was grossing over $400,000 a week in advertising revenues. With the promise of an heir apparent, NBC had managed to sell the show out for Johnny's debut, there were twenty-nine sponsors on an alternating basis. In addition to the money, NBC also promised Johnny a free hand in running the show. Discounting the assurances of politicians, the most ridiculous promises in the world must be those of television executives guaranteeing artistic freedom to an entertainer. NBC is certainly no exception to this rule, as Johnny was to soon find out.

As Paar's days as host dwindled, one of his last guests was billed as a mystery guest, and turned out to be Johnny's sister. Leave it to Paar to give us the only glimpse of Johnny's family on the "Tonight Show."

Finally October 3 arrived and the first Johnny Carson "Tonight Show" went on the air with guests Rudy Vallee, Joan Crawford, Tony Bennett, and comedy writer Mel Brooks. For those holding their breaths, it was an average show, typical of what was to follow. The lack of sparks led some to predict early foreclosure on Johnny's lease on the desk. NBC said they would wait and see. What they were waiting to see were the ratings. When they finally got a look at those numbers, several dozen executives breathed sighs of relief—Johnny was holding the audience that Paar had had.

Before the first air date Johnny had gone to Yankee Stadium dressed as a Yankee and pitched batting practice to Mickey Mantle, Roger Maris, and Elston Howard. The film of this was aired the first week. Unlike Paar, but in the footsteps of Allen, Johnny had decided to get out from behind the desk more often. Soon after, he would fly with the Air Force aerobatic team, the Thunderbirds. One wag termed him "The George Plimpton of his day." The early days of the Carson "Tonight Show" continued in that vein, with the usual run of guest celebrities–Tallulah Bankhead, Count Bassie, Mitch Miller, Andy Williams, etc., parading to the couch. This was interspersed with an assortment of All-American teams, odd balls, and strange gadgets.

When asked what he thought of Carson's version of the "Tonight Show," Paar said he went to bed early, but what he had seen he liked. Jack did not go on to say how he managed to wrestle his ego into bed while his successor carried on from his old chair.

In the early stages, Johnny found he would have to deal with the constant complaint heard by every host of the "Tonight Show"–too many commercials. After Steve Allen and Jack Paar had presumably put the issue to rest, Carson was called on to do the same once again. To what purpose no one is quite sure because the one true constant standby on the "Tonight Show" has been the commercials. If you have missed Allen, or Paar, or Carson justifying the commercials, don't worry, you'll probably have the opportunity to see the next host go through the whole thing again.

Paar sent Johnny a telegram opening night and that appears to be the last warm contact the two have had. Several months after Johnny's first show, Oscar Levant appeared on one of Paar's specials. The conversation eventually got around to the "Tonight Show" and the new host. Levant said that he had watched the show and found Carson, "Very amiable about being dull."

In a rare counterattack, Johnny charged Levant with watching the "Tonight Show" on radio and being "obviously sick."

Despite an occasional cutting remark aimed at politicians, such as his observation that after losing the California gover-nor's race Richard Nixon was now going to ". . . run for head of his family," the majority of Johnny's grief came from those offended by the off color tint of some of his material.

While he and physical fitness expert, Debbie Drake were lying on adjoining mats in preparation for an exercise demonstration, Johnny turned to her and innocently quipped, "Do you want to leave a call?"

More than a few letters arrived at NBC concerning that incident, and one columnist criticized him for it. Johnny was forced to go on the air and explain that the show would get pretty dull if he could not do something racy every now and then, if that is what the remark was considered.

As 1963 got underway, NBC, with a watchful eye on the rating numbers, was finally satisfied. Not only was Carson keeping the Paar audience, he was adding to it with huge chunks of new audience every night. By March he was reaching 500,000 more homes than Paar had been reaching the previous year. Even NBC was amazed because of the blandness of the show in comparison to the histrionics of the Paar regime. Not only that, but Allen was pulling over a million in audience in competition and still, Carson's version of late night fare was outselling Paar.

Delighted, the executives called Johnny in and signed him up to a new contract for the coming year. He had showed them new and bigger numbers, and he had done it without controversy. Playing it for laughs, he had hit upon a nerve in videoland and millions stayed up to laugh with him.

Some measure of his jump in status came as a house subcommittee investigating the effects of ratings on programming, called him to Washington to testify. What Johnny said, having seen both sides of the coin, was essentially that, if the ratings are good, so is the system; if they're bad, ratings destroy your show.

Back in New York the show was getting more structured. Slowly the format we now know as the "Tonight Show" was evolving. Johnny found that talking to guests before the show had a tendency to take the edge off what they had to say, so he seldom sees them before they are on the air.

With no "television family" of the type Paar had, Carson had to develop ongoing bits that could be dug out when the situation required—meaning, when all else failed. One of these is the endless argument Ed and Johnny have concerning the relative intelligence of pigs and horses. It is a far cry from the Berlin Wall, but as they say, "It sells!" At one point, they went as far as to bring a trained pony and a trained pig on the show to resolve the question. The pig sang and the pony counted with his hoof. The argument continues to this day.

When asked about Paar recommending him for the job, Johnny now says, ". . . I'd heard reports of that, but I really don't know."

Paar then said in a magazine interview that Carson hung around Paar's studio at NBC to find out how he was doing on the "Tonight Show." Incredulous, Carson went on the air and explained that that was not the case at all. "It's not a question of a feud. I merely want the truth known." Johnny could not believe the entire episode had happened. He found dealing with Paar "like arguing with children."

Nowhere was the difference between the two men made more obvious than in the manner in which they each handled guests. One night Red Buttons launched into a particularly virulent political tirade. Whereas Paar might have goaded him on into saying almost anything, Carson merely waited for Buttons to stop for air and said, "You're sort of a redheaded Albert Schweitzer tonight aren't you?" Red got the message. It was time to stop being topical and start being funny. Being topical would be OK on the show, after all Johnny's monologue is based on it, but like the monologue, the topical material would best be presented within a comedy routine, a la George Carlin, Albert Brooks, etc.

Despite the ever-climbing audience numbers and the sky-rocketing advertising grosses, Johnny still got an inordinate panning from the press. Most of it was aimed at his failure to become another Paar, which he had never set out to do in the first place. The complaints took many forms, but mostly they accused the guests of being decidedly second rate. In addition, they did not like Johnny's ability to turn almost anything into a double entendré, claiming that "his lewd and sly glances offend the sophisticated." John Crosby went so far as to say: "He exhibits all the charm of a snickering small boy scribbling graffiti on a public wall." Not content that he had made his point, Crosby continued: "All Carson's schtick

107

is done with no apparent gift for the performing arts."
Johnny bridled at this type of criticism. If he was that bad,
why do all those millions tune in every night?

To explain his own approach to the "Tonight Show" he
said, "Paar works emotionally. I work intellectually. Controversy is easy. I could make every front page in the country
tomorrow by knocking Kennedy or coming out in favor of
birth control." And taking a stand like that was the only
thing Johnny was not about to do. He would have people on
from time to time to present divergent points, but John
would always remain neutral, except in the most obvious
cases of injustice.

In August of 1963 Johnny and Joanne Copeland were
married. She was twenty-eight, he thirty-eight. In talking
about her new husband Joanne said, "He made me alive. . . .
He showed me a whole new world." Sutton Terrace was still
Johnny's address.

Soon after the marriage Johnny signed to do his first
movie, "Looking For Love" co-starring Connie Francis and
Jim Hutton. But the picture was shelved because of conflicting schedules and waning interest. Except for brief shots of a
television set showing the "Tonight Show" as part of a scene,
Johnny has yet to appear in a motion picture. Every year or
two rumors that John is going to make a motion picture
circulate, and Johnny has always said he would be available
for the right property, but so far nothing has materialized.
There certainly is no celebrity with bigger box office
potential.

The "Tonight Show" continued to enjoy success as
Johnny settled into his new married life and stopped spending a lot of time in the bars. At one point NBC felt obliged to
warn Johnny about what had become known around the
show as "anxiety binges," which were prompted mostly by
the continuing pressures of the show. Either the warnings
took, or his marriage stopped them, or he just simply out-
grew them; whatever the case, he cut his alcohol consump-
tion to a much more moderate level, and almost became a
recluse in his home with his new wife. Carson readily admits
that alcohol acts very quickly on him; it takes only one or

two drinks for him to become tipsy. "I don't drink anymore. I had a tendency to get hostile, so now I leave it at a bottle of beer or an occasional vodka and tonic."

In early 1964 Johnny signed to play for four weeks at the Sahara hotel in Los Vegas, at $40,000 a week. He put a great deal of preparation into the night club act and when he took his summer vacation in July, it paid off with record crowds. The first two nights he played to a to-night total of 2,999 paid covers, breaking the old Sahara record set by the immortal Judy Garland. The act was completely new. He used none of the material from the "Tonight Show." Instead, he lampooned TV and commercials, something he could never do on the air. He did comedy bits, which were very well received by reviewers, especially the kiddie shoe emcee with a hangover. Also on the big bill were John Bubbles and January Jones.

By the end of his run at the Sahara, Las Vegas knew what the television execs found out a year earlier—Johnny Carson spelled big audiences. He was given a contract that provided for Las Vegas appearances whenever he was off from the "Tonight Show" for the following three years. He was also booked to play a week in Lake Tahoe. Not only was he rapidly becoming the biggest name in television, but Carson was making moves toward becoming a giant headliner on the club circuit as well.

Johnny Carson had never been a stranger to work, but the combination of club dates and an unrelenting schedule for the "Tonight Show" were having the same effect on him as they had had on Paar. This, combined with a popularity that tends to encourage fans to attempt an overfamiliarity not welcomed by John, led to even more tension. He began to snap at questions about his secretiveness.

"I'm friendly, aren't I?" he would shoot back when it was pointed out that he did not seem to fit into the public's idea of what a star should be. "I'm polite, aren't I? I'm honest! All right, my bugging point is low, I'm not gregarious. I'm a loner. I've always been that way!"

The pace was eating him up, and this was exactly what he had said years before that he would have to guard against. He

109

could not do it though; he felt uneasy about delegating authority because of his experiences with the CBS "Johnny Carson Show." Instead of letting up, he took on more of the production decisions and functions himself. He was trading his own nerves for bigger numbers, and the numbers were big—$18,000,000 in advertising revenue by mid-1964, and the show was sold out for a year in advance.

It was becoming difficult to find Johnny anywhere, except on the television, as he increasingly locked himself away from all but the people he worked with and his wife. To an extent, there was some justification for his fear of personal contact with the public. Most of his contacts had resulted in near disasters.

The first thing Johnny found out about being a celebrity was the personal demands it put on him. "Am I not entitled to a private life? I can't go anywhere without being bugged by somebody. I'd love to just hike out down the street, or drop into a restaurant, or wander in the park, or take my kids somewhere without collecting a trail of people. But I can't." He became almost resentful of his own stardom. "Wherever you go, some clown grabs you and demands an autograph; it's a pain in the butt. . . . I've had a guy in a urinal ask me for an autograph!"

Many Americans view Johnny Carson from their bedrooms and therefore feel more familiar with him than they might with another celebrity. However, some people carry this feeling of familiarity to extremes, such as the man who once came over to a table John and Ed McMahon were sharing in a better supper club. This was no ordinary man, he stood over six feet six inches tall, and Johnny estimates he must have weighed well over 280 pounds, dwarfing even Ed, who is no small fry.

"I want you to come on over and see some friends of mine Johnny," said gorilla man as he reached down, not waiting for John's reply, and took his elbow and forceably brought him to his feet.

"Really, I'd rather stay right here." said John, whose first impulse was to paste him in the mouth. He didn't because of the obvious publicity, but also, he realized as he stood that the man had consumed enough liquor to put even Ed under the table.

"Come on!"

"No. Really I don't. . . ." Johnny could not even get the words out as he was dragged over to a table of twenty people.

"Folks, I'd like you all to meet a friend of mine, Johnny Carson. Say hello to my friends, John!"

"Hello." With that, John turned and started back to his table. He made it as far as the 280 pounder's arm would allow. There he came to an abrupt halt, as a gorilla hand grabbed him by the nape of the neck and dragged him back to the table.

"Where you going little man?" With that he let go of Johnny and putting two fingers in his mouth, whistled for the band to be quiet. "Hey! You guys want to knock it off! Johnny Carson here is going to entertain my friends."

There certainly was no way he was going to fight his way out, so he continued to try to reason with the man. "Please, I'm a very busy man and I have to get up early in the morning."

Grabbing John by his jacket lapels, the giant lifted him clean off the ground. "But I promised my friends."

By now Ed had made his way to the table and managed to get him back down on terra firma where John said, "I'm very sorry but I have to leave."

"Where ya going," the man shouted to the rapidly departing Carson, "There ain't nothing else open!"

"My house is," replied Johnny, who was half out the door already.

Big, burly drunks are only one small group of people who want something from John. Most people want an audition a niece, an aunt, or a son. Like the woman who grabbed him from an alley one night, she had a son who she wanted John to see so badly that she hid in an alley waiting for Johnny to pass. When he finally appeared, she managed to grab his shoulder, spinning him completely around.

"I want you to hear my son sing!" She reached back into

111

the dark recesses of the alley and produced her son, who she shoved in front of Johnny, "sing Albert!"

Johnny remembers that one well, "and he sang . . . right there in the street."

The pressure on Johnny was not eased any by the beginning of his feuds with the executive corps at NBC. During the political conventions of early 1964, Johnny found his "Tonight Show" playing stepchild to the news departments, which interrupted the show with convention news no matter how insignificant. Carson countered by alluding to Huntley and Brinkley as a comedy team.

Robert Kintner, the NBC vice-president in charge of news who believes television news to be second in importance only to air and food, heard the comment and went straight through the roof. The reverberations were easily heard in the "Tonight Show" offices. Kintner layed down the law: "No more lip from Carson . . . or else!"

It was time to see just how big a star John had really become. This was to be the first of many power plays. NBC, for some reason, has always thought Johnny could not add numbers. He could, and did. The numbers he read said that he was making more money for NBC than the news. With that in mind, his monologue for the next night's show was entirely taken up by a witty lampooning of the television news coverage of the conventions. Because the "Tonight Show" is taped in the early evening, NBC has a choice to make. Either go with Kintner and refuse to air the monologue, or back down, acknowledging Carson's position as something other than the host of an NBC stepchild program. The monologue was aired and Kintner was forced to back off. Carson had won his first confrontation, but in the process, he had not made any new friends.

By late 1964, the "Tonight Show" had become so popular that NBC decided to go with taped reruns on Saturday nights, making Sunday the only Carsonless day on the calendar.

Six nights of Carson lasted only a little while, as Johnny realized that he could not keep that pace much longer and also stay out of a rest home. He decided to take part of his vacation by remaining absent from the program on Mondays. Around the show business community it was made a joke that Johnny never showed up on Monday, but out there in TV land, it was no joking matter. The audience was tuning in to see Johnny and was quite upset when he failed to appear. The deluge of letters pouring into NBC forced Johnny explain on the air that NBC owed him vacation time from the previous years and he was taking it on Mondays. The explanation was fine, but to this day people are reluctant to grant him even one day off. When they turn that set on, the viewing public does not want to know *why* he is not there. Slowly but surely, however, the public is getting used to these absences, which have increased every year so much so that it seems to be a fifty-fifty chance that Johnny will be host for his own show.

With his entry into the big time, Johnny began to cut some of his links with the past. He loved the towns he grew up in and several times went back to visit. It never worked out for him though. "I would have had the time of my life seeing the old places and the old faces again, but the attitude of the people was, 'I guess you're so big we bore you now.' What was I supposed to say to that? Agree with them? They'd be furious. But if I said I was enjoying myself, they'd say I was being condescending." Asserting that success has not spoiled Johnny Carson, he explains, "I don't think it's you that changes with success—it's the people around you who change. Because of your new status, they change in relation to you."

Apparently one person who did not change is Al Bruno, Carson's manager who "found" him, moved him from West Coast to East, and managed him through his career today. Al Bruno had early seen Johnny's talent for making the most rigid script appear spontaneous and had booked him on a myriad of talk shows and game shows, eventually landing him on the granddaddy of them all: the "Tonight Show."

Had Johnny been aiming for a few weeks on "Hollywood Squares" with several guest appearances on "What's My Line," Bruno would probably still be his manager. But as one of Johnny's associates says, "Johnny is a person of tremendous growth and people who don't grow with him, don't stay with him." Bruno did not stay.

Neither Johnny nor Bruno will discuss Carson's dismissal of Bruno, so a concrete explanation for it is hard to come by. More likely than not, it was not any single incident, but rather an accumulation of ineptness that led to the parting. Once, while appearing with his nightclub act at Miami Beach's Eden Roc Hotel, the intricately taped sound effects that went with Johnny's act became snarled during the show for three consecutive nights. The results were disasterous; no one laughed, and for a comedian there *is* no greater disaster. Bruno was directly responsible for the technical aspects of the act, and John called him after the third laughless night. Enraged to the point of tears, he melted the telephone lines between Florida and New York. ". . . This is it!! The end of the road, Al!!!!" He slammed the phone down and that *was* the end for Al Bruno.

Bruno had made other mistakes, most of which were financial, such as the reputed deal Budweiser beer had offered Carson. Johnny would do their commercials, and Budweiser would give him a distributorship in return. Bruno turned it down, cold. The deal sounded good to Johnny, and he told Bruno. Still, Bruno said no, cash or no deal. The people at Anheuser Busch shrugged their shoulders, and offered the same deal to Sinatra, who jumped on it. That distributorship turned into a multi-multimillion dollar property.

In explaining Bruno and several other people Johnny had fired, Ed McMahon said, "Johnny gets angry at ineffectual, inefficient people who don't do their job properly. It bugs him when people don't pull their own oars."

Johnny looked at the star he had become and then at his bank balance. He might as well have been a middle executive in a large corporation because all his success had not translated into financial security of any kind. He bought out the rest of Bruno's contract and looked for someone who was better equipped to advise him in both career and money matters. He would find some help with new lawyers, but it was not until several years later that he found Sonny Werblin, who gave a unified course to his career.

The Old "Tonight Show" had started at 11:15 in New York because that is when Ruppert beer, the major sponsor, wanted it to start. The days of Ruppert beer's sponsorship had long passed, but the tradition of starting at 11:15 persisted, despite the fact that many stations chose to run their news programs until 11:30 and pick up the network "Tonight Show" at that time. The NBC-owned local station in New York and many other locals did this. The practice bothered Johnny since he had lobbied long and hard to get the first fifteen minutes dropped from the show. NBC steadfastly said no. More stations found fifteen minutes insufficient for the news and extended it to thirty, including the local in San Francisco. No one bothered to tell John that his largest West Coast audience and his largest East Coast audience were missing his monologue. He found out when sitting in his dressing room before a show, almost two weeks after the fact. The course of action for John was a simple one. He would not do his monologue until the local networks in New York and San Francisco picked up the show at 11:30.

On February 20, 1965, when most viewers expected Johnny to walk briskly through the curtains, out popped Ed, explaining that Johnny was "late," but was expected any minute.

Sure enough, promptly at 11:30, out came Johnny, "Welcome to the winter of my discontent." Ed had covered nicely, but John was not about to lie to his audience. He explained his "fifteen-minute virus." It was not that he, or any of the people who worked on the show, thought that the monologue was going into a time capsule. A lot of people had put many hours of work into it, but as things stood now, with the major markets running news programs until 11:30, "The monologue is now seen by four Navajos in Gallup, New Mexico and the Armed Forces Radio."

This was all part of the continuing feud between Johnny and the executives at NBC, who still refused to acknowledge the "Tonight Show" as their biggest money-maker. They were getting Johnny cheap, and they dealt with him cheaply. When the newsmen got up to the executive floors to ask what was to be done about the "first fifteen," one of the vice presidents pooh-poohed the entire incident by saying, "Don't worry. He's going to be called in and shown the "facts of life" in his NBC contract."

He was called in, and after another night of absence from the first fifteen, he went back to the old time for a short period. Soon, the responsibility for that segment of the show fell to Ed McMahon, creating still more problems. It was not for a full two years that NBC managed to get all 211 network stations lined up and aired for the hour and a half we now see.

It was time for new domestic surroundings as well. John and his new bride Joanne bought a co-op in a building in the United Nations Plaza, the same building that housed Truman Capote and Robert Kennedy, The move was completely handled by the petite Joanne, who had by this time taken up interior design. Moving a man like Johnny might seem a problem. Not so says Joanne, "When we moved, Johnny said, 'Don't worry about my things. I'll pack them myself.' So he opened a closet and looked in, and there were his water skis, telescope, guitars, bowling ball, tennis racquet, scuba gear, swim fins, drums (name anything you can't pack), bow and arrow, straw target." She continues relating the story, still amazed with her husband. "He looked at it for five minutes, turned around and said, 'Hokay,' and that was that."

Interests he had outgrown were left behind; now he spent his weekends on his small boat, the "Deductable" (which he was always quick to point out, "It isn't").

By now Johnny was so popular that Westinghouse Broadcasting, who owned the syndicated "Merv Griffin Show," ran the "Tonight Show" before the "Merv Griffin Show," realizing the futility of competing with Johnny.

In most markets, Merv was competing with the "Tonight Show" along with ABC's entry into the late night market, the "Les Crane Show." Together they hardly put a dent in Carson's ratings. Rather, they fought between them for the scraps that fell from the "Tonight Show" table. Soon Crane

116

was cancelled. The show relied heavily on Crane's abrasive personality and his ability to foment controversy. His cancellation seemed to prove what Johnny had been saying all along, "I am not a fan of those shows and I think their whole approach is a substitute for talent. They insult people. They're rude, and it embarrasses me to watch." They must have embarrassed more people than just Johnny.

But the rush was on. Johnny had shown them the trail to the pot of gold, and every network and producer of syndicated shows, and half the local stations across America brought out their own version of a talk show. Some made pretentions at originality, but most were merely poor copies of the "Tonight Show," and they were usually just as good as the "Tonight Show" is without Johnny. In addition to Merv, ABC cleaned up Crane's act and brought him back in hopes of luring some of the gold away from NBC. For Les Crane it ended in the same way. But he was only the tip of the iceberg; battalions of talk show hosts followed in the next ten years. Only one network survived the "Tonight Show," and only two syndicated shows stood the test of time: Merv and Mike Douglas. Both Merv and Douglas drew their support mostly from daytime audiences, Johnny's old bailiwick, instead of daring to run the gauntlet of late-night competition with Carson.

In explaining the popularity of the talk show, Johnny sees no mystery in their ability to draw millions to television sets every night. He says, "It's only natural. After all, everything else on TV is adapted from another medium. The big time talk show is peculiar to TV." He has acknowledged that Paar might have been more exciting than he is, but that obviously is not the name of the game since John has always managed to set a higher rating than Paar. One thing both Carson and Paar recognized about television is its assets and limitations and how these qualities could be best used on a talk show. "It's a sense of immediacy," Carson says. "You feel that what you are watching is going on now, and you are included, rather than merely a spectator."

The essential ingredient in all talk shows is the guest list, which is basically the same for all shows, allowing for those particular favorites of one show or another. Therefore, there should not make much difference which show you watch. After all, George Carlin is George Carlin, no matter where you see him. Not quite. Entertainers reach a level of performance on the "Tonight Show," especially when Johnny is there, that simply is not attained when they appear on other shows.

Many of the truly funny men love playing to Carson. Woody Allen likes appearing with him rather than other hosts because, "He's not out there fighting to get lines. He loves it when you score, and he's witty enough to score himself."

Carson always seems able to come up to the standards set by that night's guest. Joan Rivers simply states, "He's *so* funny." And in turn Joan is seldom anything but *so* funny when she's on with Johnny. He plays well with other comedians, usually heightening their routines with prepared straight lines delivered as if spontaneous.

Johnny may top a guest, but never does he step on laughs. Dick Cavett, who used to be a writer for Carson, notes, "He seems to have an uncanny instinct for knowing when you're going for a laugh."

However, not everyone feels that warmly about sitting down with Johnny and trying to be funny. One well-known comic hates appearing with Carson. "You tell a joke and Johnny repeats it, scavenging, hunting all over for the last vestiges of a joke, trying desperately to pull a laugh of his own out of it."

Another "Tonight Show" regular who cannot stand the pressure under Carson (yet still does the show) says, "I'd much rather be on anybody else's show. Johnny doesn't talk to you very much. He waits. He knows how to save you, but he just doesn't want to. Everything he says is considered. You could do it by mail."

Johnny is quite often criticized for not bailing guests out when they bomb. He merely shrugs his shoulders and explains, "It was their fault for bombing in the first place." When a guest starts to bomb, Johnny's main concern is the show, and saving face for the guest is way down the list of priorities. Usually John will throw a little gas on the guest as he goes down in flames. Better a fireworks display than a boring show. If the guest is obviously putting the audience to sleep, Carson will pantomime dozing, jolt himself awake, shrug, look at the audience, and if that does not work he will keep looking until he finds a vein of laughter. Usually, it does not take him too long to find it. "If they bomb," Johnny says, "Have some fun with it." Unfortunately, most performer's egos will not allow them to see it that way, but in the end, this is what keeps the show at the top of the ratings. Johnny always finds a way to make it light and keep it moving.

For some performers, however, this can be more than merely egg on the face, as in the case of Jackie Mason who says of his appearances on the "Tonight Show," "The first time I appeared on the show, Carson seemed to like me very much. But the next time he resented me. Maybe he thought I was putting him down. I really don't know. But each time Carson looked at me, it was with undisguised alienation and contempt. I kept gabbing and Carson's expression was now one of nausea. He has never invited me back. I'd never go back again, even if he asked me." Even after that broadside, Mason still pays Johnny his due, "He has a great idea of taste and balance, and he's a master at keeping the show in a light vein. Carson is perfect at what he does."

There is an old joke that says that there are three things all men believe they can do better than any other man. 1) manage a baseball team, 2) build a fire, and 3) make love. Hosting the "Tonight Show" is a job that should have a place on that list. Everyone seems to have his own opinion about how Johnny should conduct the show. The complaints about his lack of topicality and controversy have tapered off in recent years, but in the first several years, they were loud and clear.

The critic, author, and actor, Rex Reed, once went so far as to say, "It has always been my personal convication that Carson is the most overrated amateur since Evelyn and her magic violin." Rex is entitled to his opinion, but the one thing Carson is not, is an amateur. Reed found, "The most annoying thing about Carson is his unwillingness to swing, to trust himself or his guests. Unlike Dick Cavett, Mike Douglas,

119

or Merv Griffin, who are all much better interviewers, Carson gauges everything by the size of the laugh and the response to the electronic applause meters. He never looks at you; he's too busy 1) watching the audience to see if they are responding, and 2) searching the face of his producer for reassurance."

All of what Reed says might be true. The one item he fails to take into consideration is that the show is not being done for Rex's amusement, or for that matter, is it really being done for the studio audience. The "Tonight Show" is done for those ten million people who tune in very night; and they do not see, and do not care about, what is going on off camera. As long as what they see is bright, lively, and entertaining, they will tune in again the next night. As Johnny has said over and over again, "That is what the game is all about."

But as Johnny headed toward his fifth year at the helm, the cry for him to become another Paar, or at the very least, become more controversial could be heard from most reviewers. In response, he tried to explain it one more time, "Sure there's some trivia, some chitchat. You can't have a special every night. I've never used the show as a forum for controversy. That's easy. You bring on a homosexual and say, 'Should we legalize homosexuality?' That's not controversy." No, it's not, but it passes for controversy on television.

Still they keep sending more hosts out in front of the cameras in hopes that one will find the key to unlock part of Carson's audience. Johnny has always maintained that there is enough to go around, "Some viewers will go for Mike Douglas, some for Merv Griffin, some for Bishop, some for me. Nobody is ever going to walk away with the whole audience. There's plenty for everyone."

Johnny said that before all those others were either cancelled or moved to the safer pastures of daytime TV. As far as the network executives are concerned, there is not enough to go around. The viewers like Johnny better, and, despite their complaints about the pressure, the performers seem to like Johnny better. They respond to his style with the best performance they can give, and most recognize that they are all

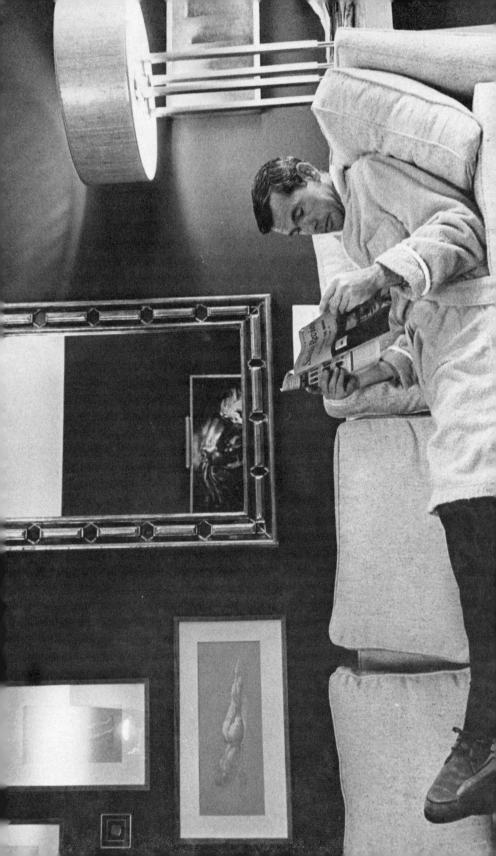

working toward the same goal: a good show. And that means more for everyone concerned: more viewers for Johnny, and more book sales, night club dates, movie roles, or record sales, et al. for the guest.

Peter O'Toole's appearance is an excellent example of how Johnny can take most anything that happens and still keep the show under control. Peter had been booked weeks in advance for an appearance on the show. In an effort to keep the commitments he had made, Peter got off the plane and went directly to the "Tonight Show" studio after three days straight of filming *Lord Jim*. After the usual glowing intro-duction, Peter sat down in the guest's seat and John started the interview. Immediately, Johnny saw that something was wrong. O'Toole could barely speak—he mumbled, and had great difficulty even making a cogent sentence. Johnny start-ed to play it for laughs, but quickly shifted gears when he realized it was not an act. O'Toole was really incapable of responding; he was stupefied with fatigue. Carson immediate-ly broke for a commercial and helped Peter from the stage, explaining to the audience that he was not drunk (as it had appears), but the actor hadn't had any sleep in well over forty-eight hours. He then brought on the other guests and covered it so well that most people were completely unaware that anything had gone wrong.

Trouble on the show has never been a problem for John; it is what he has been training himself for since his first magic trick. However, trouble from the cost accountants, execu-tives, and those outside the show are what he has the greatest difficulty handling. Around Christmas of 1965, Federal Com-munications Commissioner, Robert E. Lee, in an effort to generate a little publicity for himself, objected to some of the material on the "Tonight Show." He was quick to point out that Johnny was a great talent. (No telling when Mr. Lee might run for office and need a "Tonight Show" appear-ance.) *But* he said, ". . . a few of the comments on the show would raise some eyebrows." What Robert E. Lee was refer-ring to was an exchange that had taken place several weeks before between Johnny and Ray Milland. Ray had explained that because of a lack of sufficient lavatory facilities on his last picture, he was forced to use a swimming pool that was on the set as a comfort station. "Comfort station" and "lavatory" were the words used by Milland that so offended Mr. Lee. Normally, a complaint such as this would be relegated to the lunatic fringe file and soon forgotten. But Mr. Lee happened to sit on the Federal Communications Commission, the regulatory agency that determines who shall be licensed, and as such demanded a reply to his suggestion that, "the networks should get together and police themselves."

Johnny came on the next night and was genuinely baffled by Lee's remarks. He explained that the show was an ad lib program, and no raciness was intended. Then, thinking of Lee's accusation of indecency, Johnny asked Mr. Lee to explain what he meant by "indecent." Robert E. Lee was at great pains to explain what he had meant, and at last admitted that he did not know what "indecent" meant. Nonetheless, that night's show reflected the power of Robert E. Lee's small mind and, contained more than the usual number of bleeps and cuts.

When Carson asked exactly what the FCC found so objectionable, the other commissioners reacted to Lee's comments with a yawn. Johnny began to push the point home, realizing how easily NBC could be stampeded into cutting his show, "I just don't see how anyone could be that petty!"

Lee began to get ripped from all sides, he was the laughing stock of all Washington. In self-defense Lee denied being petty. In fact, he went on to say that he was known as the best teller of dirty stories in the entire District of Columbia. That was all Johnny needed. Offended, he came on the show and aimed at Mr. Robert E. Lee. The target was imposing, and shooting at it has to be the dream of every artist who feels restrained by the legions of busybodies always ready to safeguard everyone else. It is not known whether Mr. Lee watched as Johnny said, "Why is it that what is fine to laugh at when told in our homes is 'indecent' when it comes over the TV. . . . Everyone wants to protect everyone else's morals from what doesn't affect them." It was the last Johnny heard from Robert E. Lee.

Despite the "danger" to their morals, the rating services

estimated that 12 million people watched the "Tonight Show" on a regular basis. The advertising revenue commanded by an audience this size was $20 million annually. Johnny's contract that originally called for $100,000 a year was long gone, replaced by one that provided for thirteen weeks vacation and $15,000 a week.

Now the acknowledged king of late-night television (at least until the next batch of challengers stepped forward in a few years), Johnny began to loosen up and even took a few pot shots at the golden goose—the advertisers. One night, as Ed scrambled back to his commercial booth to deliver his pitch for Smuckers, he was unaware that Johnny had followed him. In his usual super-professional manner, Ed had dipped out a huge scoop of vanilla ice cream, dropped it into a plate and was ladeling the mouth watering, sugary fruit topping onto it in giant gobs.

"How long will that take to melt?" said Johnny as he stepped up to the startled McMahon. Unflappable as ever, Ed continued with the pitch. "Sure looks good." Johnny pressed on, "Why don't you have some?" Then Ed explained that he had just eaten and knowing there was no way to stop Carson now, tried to wrap it up as soon as possible. But Johnny continued, "You've been talking about how wonderful it is. It does look wonderful on television." There was no way out and McMahon finally admitted that the "ice cream" was, in reality, lard. Ice cream would melt under the hot studio lights and therefore they had to use a substitute.

"There ought to be a certain amount of honesty, you know," said John as he returned to his seat behind the desk. He was rolling now, "When they show that woman cleaning that floor and say, 'One swipe to it,' did you ever see that floor? It's the filthiest thing you have ever seen and they go right through. . . . They put graphite on the floor, powdered graphite. . . . I don't think that's fair!" Neither did the audience, and they screamed their approval. But the advertisers did not approve. It looked as if Johnny was going to bloody a few of the noses Paar had hit so often, but that was not to be the case. As always, John let us know he was well aware of what was going on, and it bothered him as much as it both-

123

ered you and me; but a steady diet of that was the surest way to get cancelled. "There's no percentage in getting involved. I'm an entertainer and this is an entertainment show." he said. "When people tune in at 11:30, they don't want to hear about civil rights." John knows the percentages better than anyone else on TV, and the largest percentage of the American audience wants entertainment.

In explaining why, unlike Paar, Carson does not make a habit of having the great celebrities on the show, he protects those percentages and says, "They're risky to the entertainment value of the program."

As guest after guest took their places on the "Tonight Show" couch, exposing details of their private lives, the public, more and more, clamored for details of the Carson's private life. Johnny became incensed and refused, "Look, I don't owe the public anything except a good performance!" The public thought differently, and the press did everything to fulfill public desire for information. But the going was rough. Johnny was not saying anything. He maintained that his stardom did not constitute the right of the public to poke into his private life. He had an absolute right to total privacy. "When Eddie Fisher was on my show, I wouldn't embarrass him by asking about his divorce any more than I would want him to ask about mine."

Ed McMahon has always explained Johnny's penchant for privacy by saying, "Johnny packs a tight suitcase." And that is the end of the subject as far as Ed is concerned.

His wife has told us that Johnny has a bowling ball and fencing foils, but who has seen him bowl or fence? The same holds true for his archery equipment, golf clubs, and snow skies. He admits to an interest in astronomy, but that is about it. He reads a lot. What does he read? He might give the name of one book, but that is all. Joanne would proudly point to the space she had to make in their new apartment for Johnny's things. Johnny has little difficulty with things; it is people in a situation has has no control over that gives him trouble. This is not unusual; there are plenty of people who cannot deal with other people, but they usually end up working with engines, or cameras, or . . . things. Things protect them from people. What is unusual is when someone like this becomes a star because of his ability to handle people as the host of a talk show. As a regular on his show says, shaking his head in amazement, "How does a buttoned up mind keep a talk show going?"

Johnny's fear of appearing shallow or uninformed stops him from in-depth probings of subjects with his guests, "I'm not equipped to talk about issues. . . . Neither was Paar for that matter." John can become incensed to the point of rage on the subject, "What the hell, I'm not the host of 'Meet the Press!' I'm an entertainer, not a commentator. If you're a comedian, your job is to make people laugh. You cannot be both serious and funny. One negates the other. Personally, I want to be a successful comedian."

There is no question, as a comedian Carson is successful, but who is this comedian? Who knows him? At the present writing, producer Art Stark, who had been with him since his days on "Who Do You Trust" said, "I'm Johnny's best friend because I'm not interested in his friendship. I don't try and make contact with him. Sometimes we go out to dinner, and if he's completely uncommunicative, I just leave."

Another staff member put it this way, "He communicates on a comedy level. *He* tells a joke and *you* laugh. He never asks people questions about themselves. It's not that he's got a star complex. He just doesn't seem interested in anyone."

Mike Zanella, who worked his way up from cue card boy to production assistant and finally talen coordinator was so totally enamored by Johnny that he decorated his apartment as a replica of Carson's. Johnny and Joanne helped him with obtaining copies of pieces they had at their New York co-op. Johnny even buys an extra article of duplicate clothing for Mike on occasion. "It was a year and a half before we had a conversation," says Mike. "When I see him on the street, sometimes I don't say hello. . . . That's the way he likes it. . . . I don't mind."

"I'm so thankful Johnny married me. I would have been a very unhappy person if he hadn't," his biggest fan, Joanne, says to open many discussions about Johnny. She does not understand all the fuss over what Johnny is like. "When he's with people he likes and enjoys, he is just like the Johnny on TV—very quick, very funny. Not on. He's not *on* when he's on TV. That's him. When he's off camera, in his office, he's under so much pressure. The show is like a party, small talk, unpredictable, a chance to see old friends."

Once Joanne threw a surprise birthday party for John, explaining to those invited, "I'm having a surprise party for Johnny and I'm inviting only the people he really likes."

"There were about eight people there," said a guest, "and I think it was a shock to all of us."

But Johnny is not that hard to know, insists Joanne, "If you have some interest in common, you can get to know him. With us it was professional football. We went to pro football games for months and we'd talk about that, then we'd talk about other things. He's shy. He's been betrayed and burned too many times." There is nothing the tiny, 94-pound Joanne would rather talk about. "Johnny's life is so full, he doesn't have time to get to know someone. The show is his life." His life was now drawing over 5,000 peices of fan mail a week, most of it, as one staff member put it, "Sex propositions, or as a second choice, tickets to the show."

For some reason, NBC felt threatened by the syndicated Merv Griffin show and began what is known in the industry as "leaning on the talent." Guests who had been regulars on both shows were told about the advantages of appearing *only* on the "Tonight Show." The message came through loud and clear—appear on Merv and don't bother coming around to the "Tonight Show." This persisted despite the "Tonight Show's" regular use of Merv's talent finds, such as George Carlin, John Byner, and Dick Cavett. The whole incident raised quite a stink, mainly because the practice is against the law. NBC quickly came out with an explanation. "Merv is not seen the same night it is taped so there is always the possibility that a guest might be appearing against himself." The more overt arm twisting stopped, but to this day, if a person's loyalty is obviously with Merv, he can look forward to reduced time on the "Tonight Show."

In late 1966 Johnny brought his night club act to the

Westbury Music Fair, in Westbury, Long Island, where he did sell-out, SRO business, with a $90,000 gross for the one-week stint.

The new year brought troubles with his first wife. Jody took their youngest son, Cory, out of his prep school in Southampton, Long Island, and brought him to Connecticut where she lived, enrolling him in public school there, in violation of their divorce agreement. John and Jody shared custody of the children, but Cory had been spending most of his time out of school with Johnny in New York. Cory went back to prep school in Southampton, and the entire incident was soon forgotten. Johnny was not about to talk about it, and Jody was not allowed to because of a clause in their divorce agreement stipulating that she does not discuss her relationship with Johnny.

With Governor Nelson Rockefeller as a guest one night, the conversation got around to Johnny living in the same building as Robert Kennedy. Rocky suggested that Johnny run against RFK in the upcoming senatorial election. Johnny laughed the suggestion off, but Rocky insisted he was serious, even when questioned by newsmen the next day. The next night on the show, John put the subject of his political future to rest, "I have no intention of running for public office. As I was saying to my wife, Joanne Bird . . . ."

Chapter Seven

In March of 1967, Johnny finally got practically everything he had ever dreamed of as an entertainer, though not by his own doing. Earlier in he year the American Federation of Radio and Television Artists, the union that controls all live and taped television and radio shows, presented its new contract to the networks. None of the demands in question affected performers or entertainers; they dealt with newsmen and announcers. AFTRA wanted more money for newsmen in New York, Chicago, and Los Angeles; they wanted to place standby announcers on FM radio stations, and reject the network rule that staff announcers must retire at age sixty-five. The networks, led by NBC, turned down the offer, and AFTRA notified their members of the rejection and called a strike starting March 28.

All AFTRA members went on strike, with a few notable exceptions. David Brinkley stayed at the helm of the Huntley-Brinkley news program to protest the inclusion of performers in what was basically an announcer's and newsmen's union, but for the most part television and radio microphones were staffed by executives, or taped repeats were aired. The "Tonight Show" used tapes reruns from the later part of 1966.

After seeing his Christmas show rerun in the middle of the spring, Johnny wired NBC and told them to stop: "I think it's all a little bit silly for what is supposed to be a live topical show. . . . Ludicrous, in fact."

NBC claimed the right to broadcast reruns and continued to do so. Johnny wanted money for the use of these repeats and again NBC said no, despite the contract that stated they could not use taped reruns without prior consultation with Johnny. John took his case to the press, "What is the price that should be paid for a rerun when it's used while your union is on strike? That's the main point. They did not negotiate with me and they still haven't. I have the right to pass judgment on reruns before they are used."

Either NBC was not listening or did not take him seriously, because the late 1966 tapes continued to be aired, causing one of his associates to remark, "Johnny thrives on topical humor. He looks like an idiot talking about Christmas."

There apparently was no way to stop the use of "Tonight Show" reruns during the strike, so John and his new adviser and lawyer, Arnold Grant, sat down to see what could be done. "It is definitely in violation of your contract with them," Grant assured Johnny, "They don't have a legal leg to stand on."

"They think they can do anything with that show," Johnny fumed. "It pays half their salaries and they still treat it like some bastard stepchild."

"What do you want to do."

"Sue them." Johnny thought for a moment, "What the hell else can we do?"

Grant knew every word in the NBC contract and had thought out many courses of action as he listened to Johnny's complaints about the way NBC treated him. "We could go for the long gamble John."

"You mean quit?"

"Not exactly quit." Lawyers are generally adept at finding a word they can use that is less threatening than what they really mean. "NBC has violated the terms of your contract with them. It is completely within your rights to rescind that contractual agreement."

"That's the same as quitting." said John.

"No. If you quit, then you are in violation of the contract, and NBC still has the legal right to hold you to the terms." Grant continued explaining the power play he had in mind, "You wouldn't be able to work anywhere else; they'd still hold the rights to you. But you're not in violation of the contract, they are." Johnny's answer was not an immediate yes. His fame notwithstanding, it was still not easy to walk away from what had taken a lifetime to achieve. "It's a chance to open the whole can of worms." Grant knew they were on solid ground, "You can get everything you ever wanted for the show. The money . . .." Johnny was still wavering, "the control. You can run it. . . . The whole works."

That was it. On April 4, one week after the strike had begun, Johnny sent a registered letter to NBC stating that he was "rescinding" his contract because NBC had used unauthorized reruns. NBC saw the handwriting on the wall from the start and leaked stories attributed to "Insiders." "It is nothing but a big money power play by Carson and his lawyers. Carson couldn't care less about AFTRA," said the "Insiders."

Grant had made his initial offers to NBC, who in turn leaked the details to the press in an attempt to sway public opinion to their side. Carson was already receiving over $700,000 a year with thirteen weeks off, and, "now the greedy ingrate was asking for a cool $1,000,000 more," was the story from "informed sources."

Carson "leaked" his side to the press. "Paar gets $40,000 a week for his one hour show; Lucy gets $3,000,000 for her series, and Gleason gets $6,000,000 for his. None of those programs make as much money for the networks as the 'Tonight Show.' "

Why NBC would attempt a press campaign aimed at turning the public away from their biggest money-maker is not clear. Carson had proved capable of running everything else off late-night TV, so this bit of contempt on the part of NBC seemed like killing the goose that hatched the money egg.

The initial effect on NBC had been one of panic, allowing Johnny to relax enough to leave the field of battle in New York to his lawyers while he and his old friend Jack Drury basked in the sun at Ft. Lauderdale, where there were almost as many reporters as hot rumors. "We're not going to get into the areas of any of their allegations or innuendos right now. We will in time," Johnny confidently told the assembled reporters. "I had been doing this show and I had been showing up every night. I haven't been playing any games with them. Now they're trying to make me look like an ungrateful wretch. As far as I'm concerned, I am now a free agent."

"What are you going to do Johnny?"

Evasive as ever, Johnny snapped back, "Let's just say I'm an unemployed prince." The reference was to his labeling himself the prince of night-time TV on his very first "Tonight Show." The headlines screamed his royalty affectation to all. NBC seized the opportunity to add more fuel to the fire.

The timing of the entire incident could not have been better. Recent surveys had indicated that total advertising revenue in the 11:00 P.M. to 1:00 A.M. time slot for all national and regional commercial spots exceeded $226,000,000 for 1966. The TV moguls had found the pot of gold. Most decent movies available to TV had been run over a hundred times, and the new movie acquisitions were being reserved for prime-time showing, leaving the network and local stations no alternative but talk shows. ABC was coming back into the market with a live Joey Bishop show, CBS was toying with the idea of Merv Griffin (now in syndication), and Bill Dana was due to come out of Las Vegas with a syndicated show. It was expected that these shows would chip away at NBC's monopoly of late-night advertisers as long as they still had Carson. Without him, the exodus from the "Tonight Show" by advertisers could turn into a stampede. NBC was reminded of this daily as the phone lines were kept busy by salesmen assuring commercial clients that it was all a political move, "Don't worry, Johnny will be back." There was no question, Johnny would never have another opportunity like this to get everything he wanted.

All eyes turned to Joey as the only definite talk show host around. He announced that his first guest would be California's Governor Ronald Reagan. The phones began to ring again at NBC, "Are you *sure* Johnny's coming back?"

After dropping the $1,000,000 figure for the press, NBC followed by stating they were not adverse to paying Carson more money. They even hinted that the $1,000,000 was not was secondary, Grant and Carson were holding out for the all important control of the show.

Jack Paar, who was no stranger to walkouts, said he felt the pressure more than likely was what had gotten to Carson, "However, if he's doing it for money, he's all wrong. But if it is for money, it's wrong to mask it. Eventually it will get him in trouble with the public."

By this time it began to look more like a money play than a matter of principle. But soon those who thought they had it all figured out began to wonder. Johnny's defenders explained to the press that his latest night club acts were so successful that he could make much more on the club circuit in just a few months than he could possibly make on the "Tonight Show."

Fine, said NBC, as they revealed the signing of comedian Bob Newhart to a contract. Without much coercion, they mentioned it was a long-term agreement calling for Bob to do several specials and pilot appearances.

"What about the 'Tonight Show'?" the press wanted to know.

"Well, he's always gotten the highest ratings of any substitute host, you know." The executive talking to the press dropped this bit almost as an afterthought.

"I wanted out at the end of this contract anyway," shot back Carson.

The switchboards at NBC lit up every morning like a Christmas tree, "Are you sure Johnny's coming back?"

"Yes."

"When?"

"Well . . . not before the strike is over." There was not much else they could say.

NBC news, understandably, was not giving much play to the Carson walkout, but CBS and ABC were have a heyday watching their giant brother squirm. Neither was above reporting the latest rumor, founded or unfounded. One rumor that kept popping up was Johnny's expected reappearance on a late-night program on CBS. It was known at this time that CBS had approached Paar with the very same idea in mind. Jack had turned them down, and now it looked like Merv would be CBS's man, but there was plenty of time for a last minute switch. These rumors were quickly put to rest by the next rumor that had NBC and CBS locked into a "gentlemen's agreement" not to pirate front-line stars from one another.

Soon the rumor of "It's only a money move," began to get more notice. Johnny prodded AFTRA to make a statement on his behalf, which they did, stating their belief Carson's action was not a money move. They were convinced that Johnny was genuinely bothered by the topicality of the rerun segments and the damage they could do to his career.

"I sent a wire to NBC at the outset of the strike protesting the reruns," John said from Ft. Lauderdale in an effort to explain his position once and for all. "But they went ahead, willfully, without my permission. They had no right to do it. The contract provides that they shall negotiate in good faith beforehand. What kind of good faith is that?" He than addressed himself to the basic philosophical dilemma of the strike, "I was required to join AFTRA in order to work for the network. I know of no business except the broadcasting industry in which a performer becomes a scab to himself and his union because of films and tape. Any other questions?"

"What about this prince thing? Do you think you're the royalty of television?" shot back one of the reporters.

"What you've forgotten," answered Johnny not too happily, "is that I had used that phrase on my first show—the night I said Paar was the king and I was just the prince. The entire reference was misunderstood."

"So when you say unemployed prince . . ."

"Let's just leave it at I'm a free agent," corrected Johnny, hoping to put the subject to rest for good.

Johnny's lawyer, Arnold Grant, confirmed Johnny's position from New York. "Johnny has taken a significant and thought-out step which relies entirely on the terms of his contract." Still, NBC was not buying it. They continued to believe that Johnny would be back as soon as the strike ended. They were prepared to give him the money, but the control of the show would remain with them.

In addition, NBC now revealed that Grant and Carson had

opened talks aimed at a new contract over six weeks ago. It was only now when they caught NBC in a "minor" misinterpretation of the old contract that they chose to squeeze the life blood out of the network, NBC retorted to Johnny's concern with the topicality of the rerun segments.

The battle raged back and forth with neither side giving an inch. The front pages of papers across America talked of little else. For the diligent reader who got past the front page, there was news of the sentencing of Bobby Baker, the financial manipulator who had almost brought Lyndon Johnson's administration tumbling down. The jury was being selected for the sensational Copolino murder trial. Someone made an assassination attempt on the vice-president of the United States, Hubert Humphrey, and Israel and Syria were in the middle of an air and tank battle on the Golan Heights. Mickey Mantle was injured as the Yankees won their opener, and the president of the United States of America was in Uruguay at the resort of Punta del Este for a summit of American States. But, much the same as when Paar had walked out seven years before, there was little else on the front pages of the news but Johnny Carson's self-imposed exile.

As April wore on into its second week, AFTRA and the networks appeared close to agreement. NBC wired Carson that the strike would, in all probability, be over by April 11. NBC also included in that wire a note informing Johnny that he was expected back at the "Tonight Show" that night. Through his lawyers, Johnny told NBC that even if the strike were ended, they should not expect him back. He had meant it when he rescinded his contract and had no intentions of appearing on a show for which he was no longer working.

It was finally beginning to dawn on the executive branch of NBC—Johnny Carson meant business. After all the talk (which NBC was used to), they realized that their worst nightmares might come true. The strike was due to end the next day and now it appeared that their biggest meal ticket had no intention of returning to the fold. It was time to stop bluffing and roll out the big guns. If Johnny Carson did not want to come back to NBC, that was one thing, but if he thought he might try earning a living somewhere else in television, he would have to guess again. NBC called in the reporters and told them that Carson faced a television freeze until his contract expired, unless he came back to the "Tonight Show" when the strike was over. "Under the terms of the contract, Carson is exclusive NBC property until 1970." They went on to say, "We have every intention of holding him to it. Which means he won't be able to do other TV work."

Extra switchboard operators had to be put on to handle the calls. The advertisers wanted out until Johnny came back. NBC frantically tap-danced while trying to juggle the many elements. On one side, there were more than a few executives with scores to settle with Carson, and they would have been glad to be rid of him for good, no matter what the cost. On the other side were the cost accountants who knew only too well what Johnny represented monetarily. Everytime any one of the executives said they did not need Johnny, the advertisers called up to ask where he would be so they could send their business where Johnny went, and then another executive would jump forward with a denial.

"We're lining up a few comedians for temporary duty on the show. . . . There's no replacement. . . . It's still Johnny's show," went the reassurances. "We'll use people on a week-to-week basis until the Carson situation is straightened out."

"What if he won't come back?"

After swallowing hard they answered, "If he won't be back, we'll get a permanent replacement."

NBC was still trotting out the Bob Newhart signing in an effort to scare Johnny back to Rockefeller Center. Each time they revealed another clause in the agreement. "In addition to specials and his own series, this new contract calls for Bob to substitute host for Johnny for six weeks each year."

What did Johnny think about all that? Nothing. He had terminated his contract with NBC, and that still stood, even though the strike was now over. He planned to fulfill engagements already contracted for. "I'm going to Baltimore on April 29. I'll be in Indianapolis for the 500 race, and I'm booked for Las Vegas in July, among other things."

Sources close to Carson said these bookings would pay Johnny $750,000 and indicated that Johnny intended to wait a week or two before attempting to settle his differences with NBC.

NBC continued to assure its advertisers, "Johnny is expected back. It's his show." But by now they were whistling in the dark. Maybe Bob Newhart was not a bluff. He was certainly the best NBC was going to do in the way of a replacement, so they continued to pump Newhart, telling the newsmen, "If we want Newhart to permanently replace Carson, we'll have to renegotiate his contract, although it does already have a provision for Bob taking over the 'Tonight Show.' "

"So Newhart is the new host of the 'Tonight Show'?" Shot back one of the newsmen.

"No!" NBC dared not say anything like that. "Right now our position could be described as watchful waiting. . . . But you can be sure of one thing—there will be a 'Tonight Show' from now on—with or without Carson."

Johnny countered by saying, "There's nothing for me to wait for. I can do whatever I want to do."

Carson's staff, by this time, had been in touch with Bob Newhart, who revealed that the contract he signed with NBC had been negotiated weeks before the strike began and had nothing at all to do with Johnny's walkout.

The first night of scheduled programming after the strike found the "Tonight" studio empty. NBC ran another tape and sent another wire to Ft. Lauderdale, this time "ordering" Johnny to return to duty on the show. Carson did not even bother to reply.

Why NBC had taken the unbelievable risk of breaking Carson's contract with the questionable use of reruns during a strike is a mystery. They obviously must have known he was bargaining hard for a better deal from NBC; Grant had been negotiating with them for over six weeks when the strike began. Handing him the weapons to beat the network, by using the reruns, when the public would have understood and sympathized with any alternative NBC might have tried, including silent movies, is difficult to chalk off to arrogance. But if it was not arrogance that led NBC to believe they could push Carson around at will, the only other acceptable answer has to be stupidity.

Now it was definite. Carson was not coming back under the terms of his old contract. NBC would have to use Newhart. They called Bob and told him the news. They did not get the elated acceptance they had expected. Newhart knew how important the "Tonight Show" could be to his career and was not about to step on Johnny's toes if it looked like the walkout was temporary. After several long distance calls, Newhart was convinced Carson held the upper hand and told NBC he had several conflicts and would not be able to make it for the first week. He would try and work out his "conflicts" in the next week and let NBC know.

The Newhart bluff had not worked for NBC and now they frantically scurried about looking for someone, anyone, who would risk going in front of the "Tonight Show" cameras. They came up with country and western singer Jimmy Dean. NBC could manage to hold some of the advertisers with Bob Newhart, but Jimmy Dean was another matter altogether. The refrain was no longer calm assurances that, "Johnny'll be back." It had changed to a note of pleading, as they tried to keep the advertisers by promising, "We'll *get* Johnny back."

The question from the advertisers was still the same, "When?"

Under Johnny's old contract NBC paid him $15,000 a week for five live and one taped (Saturday) show. Half went directly to Johnny and half to Stage "C" Productions, Johnny's own company which did some of the production work on the show. Everyone working on the show, with the exception of Ed McMahon, Milton Delugg, the band leader at that time, and Dick Carson, Johnny's brother and director of the show, were on Stage "C" payroll. The other three were under direct contract with NBC.

As NBC prepared to go with the Jimmy Dean "Tonight Show," they found there was no one to run the show.

Johnny had pulled everyone under contract to Stage "C" off the show; this included producer Art Stark, all the writers, the talent coordinators, and office staff. In effect, Johnny had left NBC with the studio, set, and name of the "Tonight Show." They had nothing.

The question of Ed McMahon's attendance at a Carsonless "Tonight Show" had been answered with a thundering silence all during the strike, but on that first night without Carson, Ed was there, in compliance with the terms of his contract. Delugg and Dick Carson were also there along with Jimmy Dean. With no preparation time, Dean did the best he could. The most charitable of the reviews said, "In poor taste." Dean cracked bad jokes about Johnny's walkout and interviewed those guests brave enough to come on and risk possible reprisals should Johnny return. Without the production staff, the job of putting on the show was practically impossible. This was dirty pool on the part of Carson according to NBC, and their bitterness surfaced as they refused to negotiate any further with Grant. NBC president, Don Durgin, demanded another representative and Grant got his old associate, Louis Nizer, who had worked so well with him during the proxy battles at 20th Century Fox that put Daryl Zanuck back in power there.

After Grant, Nizer, and Carson reviewed the entire situation, they decided to let NBC take a few audience samples, just to give them an idea of how much the new Joey Bishop Show was cutting into their audience. What NBC saw in those numbers must have chilled their souls. Joey was topping everything else on the air put together, pulling almost the same ratings as Carson had when he was on the "Tonight Show." As the week wore on, Merv Griffin's syndicated show began to move up along with the Bill Dana syndication out of Las Vegas, pushing the "Tonight Show" all the way to dead last on the charts. The numbers looked like this: Bishop 40 percent of the audience, Jimmy Dean 12 percent.

NBC had to do something fast, and with those audience numbers it would be difficult to find someone willing to put a public service announcement on the "Tonight Show." The majority stockholder of NBC, David Sarnoff, stepped in and tried to clear the air with a press conference. He explained that in the end it always boiled down to the same thing–money. In a magnanimous mood, Sarnoff said, "Johnny Carson will be accorded the courtesy of returning to the show without prejudice to the negotiations now going on." Johnny did not take him up on the offer. Getting involved in the dispute, especially on the part of his own company, carried its own special risk for Sarnoff. He has since confided to Johnny on a number of occasions that Mrs. Sarnoff is Carson's biggest fan, and her attitude remained the same throughout: "For goodness sake, David, pay him the money."

NBC was now ready to negotiate with Carson in earnest. As Durgin opened the proceedings with Nizer, he soon realized he would have been better off if he had hammered out an agreement with Grant. Before Nizer would even start to talk about a new contract, he informed Durgin that the main reason for his being brought in was to handle the trial aspects of the case.

"Trial?" Durgin was baffled by this development.

"We have already rescinded the old contract," Nizer said, noting that Durgin was not going to like what he had to say, "and we're now preparing to sue for breach." Durgin knew, with Nizer's flare for publicity, there was no way NBC could come out of a law suit smelling good.

Four days after Nizer was called in, the negotiations were going well enough for Johnny to tell the press, "There's a chance I might go back to the 'Tonight Show' this week." The salesmen ran to the phones, herding all of Johnny's sponsors back to the "Tonight Show" corral. "It depends on whether NBC and my representatives can work out our differences. If they do there is a possibility that I will return to the show. They would like me to come back and I would probably do so if everything is all right."

It was the first positive statement Johnny had made since he had "rescinded" his contract. Cracks were beginning to show in NBC's defense. They were beginning to give in on point after point. They had not completely capitulated, and that was what Carson was holding out for.

The reporters sensed the blood and pushed for more of a story, but Carson was as guarded as ever. "Did you get the big money, Johnny?"

"Money was not the main consideration, although, naturally, this always comes up."

"How much are you going for, Johnny?" As always, the newsmen wanted answers John was not prepared to give.

"I'm sorry, I can't give you that figure right now."

"Are you asking for anything else?"

Here was the crux of the issue. He could get money from almost anywhere; it was the other points where the negotiations had been hard. "There might also be some changes in personnel on the program," John hinted.

Before the walkout, John Carson had been an employee of NBC. He was now asking to become an independent contractor, with total control of the content of the show. On the money issue, there was little debate. Johnny was payed less than a million dollars a year for doing a show that grossed well over $20 million a year and cost next to nothing to produce. NBC knew they were getting him cheaply and were willing to give up some of the lucre, especially since they knew it was not the show itself that drew the ratings—it was Carson. On the other points NBC was not as willing to give, but soon did. Under the old system, Johnny had to pay for substitute hosts. NBC now did. Johnny was no longer docked for sick days, and he now got vacation pay. He won the right to raise salaries and choose his own writers, directors, and producers. In paragraph after paragraph of a contract that took up reams of paper, it was spelled out exactly where NBC had a say and where Johnny had control. The last point of contention was producer Art Stark. If NBC let Johnny fire him and replace him with his own man, they would, for all practical purposes, turn over the entire show to Carson. Johnny held firm on that demand and finally, prodded by the ever-worsening ratings, NBC gave in. Stark was fired and Johnny became the boss. With Stark gone and a figurehead in his place, Johnny was now the producer.

"Reliable sources" reported that the new deal was for $4,000,000 over a three-year period. Included in the settlement was a $1,000,000 life insurance policy and a salary reputed to be better than $30,000 a week. Plus, NBC agreed to pick up the tab for a lot of the show expenses that Carson had been paying for out of his own pocket. Another clause in the contract, revealed by NBC, was a provision prohibiting either Johnny or NBC from revealing any part of the contract.

For NBC the entire episode had the feel of dejà vu. Carson had basically followed Paar's example and had gotten the same results from NBC. There were other similarities, including the lack of love both inspired in the front offices. Paar had made an "irrevocable" decision to quit, and Carson, in the beginning, said he would "never" return. But when the meal was big enough, they both sat down at NBC's table again.

Grant said, when it was all over, "Johnny had a lot of grievances and this was a complete rewrite of his old contract."

And Durgin, in his best business polite language, said, "We are delighted at Johnny's return and we know that the feeling is shared by millions of viewers throughout the country who enjoy his unique brand of humor and intimate warmth. All of us look forward with pleasure to seeing him regularly again."

Aware that the key to his success had been the audiences' ability to identify with him, Johnny gave a carefully worded statement to the press; after all, there are not too many people in TV land who can identify with $4,000,000. "I'm grateful to the many, many people who have been kind enough to say they missed me. Television makes friendships possible with a host of unknown persons. I hope to repay their generosity with the very best that is in me." The sentiments were surely meant, but they sounded strange coming from a man who had just hired a limousine to whisk him from apartment to studio to avoid any contact with those "unknown friends." This, however, was still one of the clauses in his new contract.

Art Stark, the sacrificial lamb, put it quite simply, "I guess it's part of the game." Stark had not been included in any of the power plays despite his insistence that he was Johnny's best friend. "I'm completely at a loss; I honestly don't know what prompted it. I don't even know what changes he could have in mind. After eleven years on the show, I think I did just about all I can do in these idiot hours."

After all the furor died down, Stark admitted that he was badly hurt by the episode, "I don't criticize him for letting me go. That was his prerogative, but I do deplore the way it was done." There had been rumors for some time that Johnny was dissatisfied with the show, but rumors are a part of the job in any high pressure situation. Still, Stark thought it best to confront Johnny with them, which he did. Stark quotes Johnny as saying, "You're one of my best friends, believe me, if I had anything in mind concerning your job, I'd tell it to you." Stark let the entire issue drop until he read the newspaper accounts of Johnny's dispute with NBC. "When I heard about that [staff changes] demand I called Carson immediately." The reply he got was much the same as before. "He just laughed and said that he didn't have me in mind. He mentioned some other staff members, and frankly I felt relieved." In all fairness to Carson, there was little else he could do. If he were to tell Stark he was being let go, Stark would return to NBC and produce the "Tonight Show" in Johnny's absence, thereby cutting into Carson's negotiating leverage.

Two days after the last assurances, Carson called Stark to his apartment. Art remembers the day, "I walked in thinking it was a routine matter pertaining to a forthcoming show." In spite of what he does for a living, John is no lover of small talk. He saw no point in making an uncomfortable situation any more so. He came right to the point, "Art, I want another producer, not associated with NBC, on the show."

There wasn't much Art could say, "OK, when do you want me to leave?"

"Right now."

Art Stark, his producer for eleven years, first on "Who Do You Trust" and then on the "Tonight Show," turned without saying another word and walked out of the apartment. Today, nearly eight years after their split, they are back on amiable terms. Stark understood that under the new system there would be no one on the show who owed allegiance to anyone other than Johnny. It was his ship now, and everyone, but everyone, was going to salute the captain.

In parting, Art gave a hint as to the pressures a show like the "Tonight Show" can generate, "There is no tougher business than meeting that nightly deadline. It's got to be the most insane job in the world, trying to come up every night with timely, provocative guests and subjects interesting to viewers. It's almost as hard on the producer as it is on the host." Now the final responsibilities for both jobs would fall to Johnny. He would get other people to do the leg work, but he would carry the burden of final responsibility. At times the pressure would build to too great a pitch and come bubbling to the surface as flashes of temper, forcing John to take more time off, but for now he was king of the territory.

In an effort to keep the high ratings he had generated in Johnny's absence, Joey had as a guest on the night of John's return the old master of the walkout, Jack Paar. Paar was bright and engaging, and when Joey allowed the show to lag, almost as a reflexive action, Paar took up the slack and ran the show himself. By the end, Paar was happily quizzing Joey about his friend Sinatra. Joey Bishop with Jack Paar as a guest might draw some viewers, but Jack Paar with Joey Bishop as a guest is not exactly a TV Special.

Over on NBC Johnny returned, somewhat self-consciously explaining his absence and cracking several bad jokes on the subject. "Now that it's Passover, it's traditional to eat unleavened bread, but I came back for more dough." The rest of the show was basically the same. At 1:00 it was decided not to put it in the time capsule, although the ratings for that night read: Johnny 41 percent, CBS late movie 22 percent, Merv Griffin 16 percent, and Joey Bishop 12 percent. If there had been any question as to why NBC had given in to all of Carson's demands, it was answered that first night back.

143

Chapter Eight

Chapter 8

On more than one occasion Johnny Carson has drawn moans, and at times boos, when he quite innocently mentioned, "I'm here, six hours a week." He was, of course, referring to the hour and a half a night, four nights a week, he spends behind the "Tonight Show" desk. Most of his fans who are well aware of the fantastic salary he receives for the show sincerely believe that six hours is all the time Johnny devotes to the "Tonight Show" in a week. Nothing could be further from the truth. The "Tonight Show" occupies the majority of Johnny Carson's waking hours. It occupies the majority of the waking hours of seventy-four other people as well. They are the producer, talent coordinators, writers, publicity men, secretaries, and office staff of Raritan Enterprises (Johnny's and Sonny Werblin's company, responsible for producing and airing the "Tonight Show" five nights a week).

Johnny Carson is so good at selling the viewing public on the off-the-cuff, ad lib format of the show, that most of them believe it is indeed as easy as Johnny makes it look. This contradiction has caused Johnny, who has always thought he has not received the proper acknowledgment for the fantastic amount of preparation and work that goes into the show, a certain dismay. There is, of course, no way out of his dilemma. If he demands that acknowledgment, he must surrender the all important illusion of spontaneity, essential to our enjoyment of the show. As with most everything in Johnny's life, the truth of the elaborate production prepara-

144

tion for the show remains a prisoner of the carefully-crafted video image Johnny has created of himself.

No show that runs as smoothly as the "Tonight Show" does so by chance. It takes preparation— lots of it. Those seventy-four people working for Raritan Enterprises put together a tightly scripted show that leaves little more than a few seconds unaccounted for. Of the "Tonight Show" staff, the writers are the most transient, their contracts are up for renewal every thirteen weeks. The number of writers varies from three to as many as five or six, with one head writer responsible for coordinating the efforts of the others.

The writers stay separate from the rest of the staff. "They resent us, maybe because we're a little smarter and we make more money," said one of them recently. Possibly, but more than likely it is because of their paranoia about someone stealing a joke or ad lib from them.

Once a new writer on the show asked, on his first day, if he could see several of the old scripts to get an idea of what Johnny was looking for. Walter Kempley, then head writer, claimed that no old scripts were kept. This is not so. Every ad lib, joke, or one liner capable of prompting only a snicker is filed, cross filed, and categorically indexed by the writers, ready to be pulled from the shelf, dusted off, and sent out to work in the next night's monologue. The writers throw nothing away; they just are not about to show it to anyone else. As Kempley said, "Any bright guy can write gags for three weeks. But then panic sets in."

"If Johnny's on a pony tonight, we use the same joke we did when he was on a giraffe five years ago." The familiar refrain among the writers is: "We'll write something new when Joey Bishop does." Joey Bishop has not written anything new yet.

Writers are paid anywhere from $25,000 a year on up, but the fatality rate makes it anywhere but a place to spend your retirement. There is little sentimentality on the "Tonight Show" staff—you either produce or out you go. Sometimes your exit cue is not delivered in the most delicate manner, as with one writer who was let go when the show was based in

New York. On Christmas day plane tickets were distributed for an upcoming trip to the West Coast. After Kempley had dispensed all the tickets he had, the writer asked where his was. "Oh, there isn't one for you Frank, you're not going." The thirteen weeks were up, and that was that. Merry Christmas Frank.

Writers report for work at 10:30 in the morning and retire to their respective offices, some doing the monologue jokes, and others working on the set pieces Johnny and Ed sometimes do between the monologue and the first guest, Aunt Blabby, Art Fern, Carnak, and the now seldom-seen El Mouldo.

In addition, there is also the Mighty Carson Art Players and other set pieces like Happiness is . . . the *TV Guide* listings, or that old standby, funny picture captions. "The show is rigidly formatted, and we have a narrow range to work in. You begin to feel like a hack, writing NBC commissary and peacock jokes or Ed McMahon drinking jokes all day long," says one of the writers who regularly complains because the material can seldom take a point of view. There are universally safe subjects to knock: Bell Telephone, the NBC commissary, and Con Edison, but much beyond that the advertisers begin to get nervous for fear the show might offend someone. In the last year, however, Johnny has knocked commercial products more than ever before, reflecting a new sense of security as the unchallenged champion of late-night TV.

Political candidates are another rough area for writers because, according to NBC's Standards and Practices Department, the network censors, all political candidates have to receive the same number of thorns in their sides.

By two in the afternoon, the head writer will take thirty jokes for the monologue into Johnny, who will select a dozen or more by three o'clock and have them placed on cue cards for that night's show. Key words and phrases are spelled out with heavy felt-tipped pens on large oaktag boards to be paraded in front of Johnny during the monologue. If you pay very, very careful attention, you can every so often see Johnny reading the cards, but it takes an experienced viewer to catch him. There is a theory that Johnny does not keep

146

the best writers around because he is at his best when the prepared material bombs. That's doubtful, but Johnny is always better than his material.

Next for the writers are Johnny's ad libs with the guests, which they come up with during a brainstorming session after the talent coordinators have prepared the questions and answers for that night's guests. All the writers assemble and go over the script, firing possible one-liners Johnny can drop if necessary.

Most writers who have worked for Johnny agree that they are treated with more respect than other members of the staff, probably because Johnny had put in time as a comedy writer and identifies more readily with them. But even the writers are not above Johnny's occasional flashes of temper or vindictiveness. If a writer is not working out, he will usually be replaced, whether his thirteen weeks are up or not, forced to stay at home drawing his pay until the end of the contract. On the other hand, Johnny has been known to force writers he is not pleased with to remain in the office for the entire thirteen weeks, turning in their daily allotment of gags, none of which Johnny will use.

Once a week Johnny meets with the writers for a brainstorming session to dream up new ideas and themes for the upcoming weeks. These meetings sometimes take place at Johnny's place and the air is one of informality. During the meetings the constant cry is for "something new," but as several of the writers complain, "They all always say they want something new, but in the end, most big performers will choose to go with the same stuff they've been doing for years; no one wants to risk a failure."

In the producer's office is a giant board with the show for that week broken up into neat little fifteen-minute squares. Reading down from any day listed will tell you who is on the show, who is confirmed, who is not, and hopefully what they will do. It is the job of the five talent coordinators to see that every square is filled, and standbys are available.

The talent coordinators hunt out talent for the show and interview the endless stream of hopefuls sent by the agents, publicity men, and personal managers. With very rare exceptions, everyone must go through at least one interview. Gerald Ford or Nelson Rockefeller would not have to go through a preshow interview, but for the rest of the world, it is a must. There is almost no way to get on the show without an agent, publishing house, or other representative who knows the ropes calling and pushing the right people. If the candidate for a guest spot happens to be appearing somewhere within reasonable traveling distance of the "Tonight Show" offices, a talent coordinator will be sent to see the act. If not, then a tape or film of the performer is requested. Assuming the potential guest passes that first encounter with the talent coordinator, he will be called in for a general interview. The talent coordinator will come to the reception area where the artist has been waiting amid a virtual sea of Johnny Carsonalia—pictures, plaques, gifts sent by the many admirers—he is then taken to a cubicle where the interviewer will offer a cup of coffee and demanding say, "Tell me about yourself?" If that unnerves him, it is meant to. Better to find the panic level is down near zero right here in the office rather than on the show. The guest is being tested, and this is where those who lisp, twitch, and freeze are weeded out, unless he happens to be a lisping, twitching, discoverer of a cancer cure. Otherwise these interesting habits and nuances that are manifested at the most inopportune moments will get a polite escort to the door with a "We'll let you know."

But if there are no obvious outward signs that you are unacceptable, the talent coordinator will press on. "You spend about twenty minutes drinking coffee and calming them down, explaining about the show. And of course everybody has this great fish they've caught that they're dying to tell about. But you dig a little and sometimes help them discover what's really interesting about themselves," one coordinator remarked. For example, someone who has worked as a mattress tester, or has the ability to talk like a frog or the talent for putting seven golf balls in his mouth at one time.

If the potential guest is accepted, his name is put on a card and pinned into one of those fifteen-minute squares on the big "Tonight Show" board in the producer's office. He is given an appearance date to return to the talent coordinators office for a preshow interview. This will result in a series of "guide line" questions with answers—the script that you and Johnny will follow on the show. Johnny will stay within those pre-arranged questions, and the guest is expected to stick to the answers he has given the talent coordinator. If Johnny deviates from that script, it is considered a compliment; he feels the guest can handle on-camera conversation without a script. If the guest deviates from the set questions and answers, Johnny considers this a surprise, and all surprises on the "Tonight Show" originate with Johnny. He will probably politely excuse himself and say something like, "And now here's Ed with good news for hungry dogs." By the time the show is back on, the guest will be comfortably seated somewhere on the couch and the next guest, who will stick to the script, is in the chair.

Four copies of the agreed upon guide line questions and answers are mimeographed—one for the guest, one for Johnny, one for the director, and one for the writers to work ad libs into.

An example of the importance of the pre-interview can best be pointed out by an exchange that occurred between Johnny and Senator Barry Goldwater in 1966. Johnny, stumbling over a question, asked the senator, "Has that ever happened to you, where you just can't get out what you mean?"

The senator smiled and said, "Yes, for three and a half months, two years ago."

It was a beautiful ad lib and it brought down the house, but spontaneous it was not; it had originally happened hours before in the pre-interview.

If someone accepted on the "Tonight Show" for the first time is in the process of a coast-to-coast promotional tour for a new movie, play, book, cosmetic line, etc., the talent coordinator will suggest that the guest make the rounds of all the local talk shows and then come back to Johnny. It is felt that the exposure will season and polish the talk show routine, and indeed it will. Most guests are able to tell the interviewer the best questions as well as the answers that get the best responses.

The "Tonight Show" staff regards a good guest as someone who shows up on time without bringing along everyone they have ever known. ("They're just here for moral support," they claim.) When on the show, the guest should do his prepared bit, sit down for the interview and "relate well" to Johnny, using only the prepared script, and then shut up.

One out of every three people interviewed is accepted for the "Tonight Show." There are many notable rejects. Joan Rivers, who is now considered an ideal guest, was turned down six times before making it to the couch. Dick Cavett, who at one time was a writer for Johnny, had to get his start on the "Merv Griffin Show."

Because it is so difficult for an unknown performer to get onto the "Tonight Show," quite a bit of pressure is applied to the talent coordinators, including bribes in almost every possible form—money, clothes, trips, drugs, and sex. Such is the power the show has to make a career. It is one of the rules of the "Tonight Show" that talent coordinators do not take gifts from managers, agents, or performers in return for auditions for the show. It was put to Craig Tennis this way when he joined the show as a talent coordinator, "If you're going to sell a spot on the show kid, make sure it's for $250,00 because that's what you're going to need to live on after you're blackballed from the industry."

The power of the talk show is such that it has fostered whole new companies to specialize in introducing hopeful new talent to talk show talent bookers. Tom Cassidy and Abbie Brown run a company like this out of Boston.

For all the numbers of performers sent to the "Tonight Show," there still are not enough to keep the fifteen-minutes squares on the weekly board filled with quality guests. The staff must spend a great deal of time looking for a new "find" on their own. Someone from the staff is assigned to see every new movie as it opens. The newspapers, magazines, and trade papers are scanned every day looking for the interesting, the unusual, or the bizarre. Celebrity Register is called once a day to see who is in town and who is expected. The newest member of the talent staff will draw the job of making the night club circuit, searching for new singers and comedians. Tennis recalls the time that it was his responsibility, "After the show was over, I usually would catch a sandwich and eat it on the way to the Drake for the supper show, then over to the Bitter End, the Improv, and finally wind up down in the Village." His working day might end as late as two or three in the morning. A plug on the "Tonight Show" being what it is, every night club owner, personal manager, and agent pushes drinks and food under his nose continually; he has to keep working to keep from falling.

There are some people, though, who would prove to be more than interesting guests and who are quite simply either blackballed or not worth the hassle involved, like Ralph Nader. Nader always has something explosive to say, but it would be hard to find a "Tonight Show" advertiser who has anything nice to say about Ralph. They are sworn enemies, and whether Johnny would like to have him on or not, the threats of commercial cancellation make his appearances on anything but public television rare.

William Kunstler's political views are unwelcome on the "Tonight Show" couch. Most of what he stands for is in opposition to the conservative Nebraska ideals of Johnny, not to mention the hundreds of demands for equal time that would flood the "Tonight Show" offices from every fringe and mainstream political group in the land after the appearance.

Dr. David Ruben, author of *Everything You Ever Wanted To Know About Sex But Were Afraid To Ask,* is usually a good guest, but at times he can get into areas deemed offensive by NBC's Standards and Practices Committee. Sex change operations and his whole-hearted endorsement of masturbation tend to set delicate ears ringing.

A most definite blackball was handed out to Robert Townsend, author of *The Peter Principle,* for his comments on nepotism. Townsend was in the middle of a condemnation of American industry for passing the scepter of power down through bloodlines with no regard for a person's abilities. He said the Fords should have gotten out of the automobile business two generations ago, "In fact, John, you've got an excellent example of nepotism right here at NBC."

"How's that?" inquired Johnny, knowing the answer but hoping for the best.

"I can envision," Townsend went on, "Robert Sarnoff taking his son to the window of his office here in Rockefeller Center, and with an expansive motion noting, 'Someday this will all be yours and you too can turn sixty million minds to mush.'" It didn't take long for the blackball to come down from the executive offices of NBC President Robert Sarnoff.

Any public glorification of drugs will also get someone blackballed from the show for good, although in recent years, there is a noticeable relaxation of this prohibition from Johnny. Either he has started smoking or has finally realized a fair portion of his audience on any given night is a little high.

In addition to those not wanted, there are guests who do not want the "Tonight Show." As Steve Allen once said, "Anyone who does a talk show starts out wanting Cary Grant and the return of Christ, but pretty soon they settle for Morey Amsterdam." Neither Christ nor Grant have ever chosen to appear; nor has Marlene Deitrich, or Rock Hudson, who openly admits, "I need a script to order a sandwich." One all-time movie great had never been on the show, though he had often expressed his admiration for Carson. With the help of his wife and Ed McMahon, Edward G. Robinson was tricked onto the show one night, not realizing he was appearing on the "Tonight Show" until he walked through the curtains. Other than those few, almost everyone the show has ever wanted, it has gotten.

The "Tonight Show" pays $320 to its guest for an appearance. Not exactly working wage to the headliners who frequent the "Tonight Show" couch, but then guests usually need the "Tonight Show" more than the "Tonight Show" needs them. When the tables are reversed, the show will spring for additional fringe benefits, airplane tickets, hotel rooms, clothes, limousines, and, when the guest is worth it, additional money. But most would gladly pay for the opportunity to plug their wares.

At 11:00 A.M. the associate producers and talent coordinators meet in the producer's office for a production planning meeting. Here they discuss ideas for future shows, always looking for the right balance and "chemistry." Balance is important for obvious reasons—five animal experts on the same night is not why most people tune in. Since balance is easier to define, it is easier to achieve. Chemistry is another matter altogether. It can mean anything from a person's ability to relate well to Johnny to the effect they might have on the rest of the guests. For example, Don Rickles and Jack E. Leonard is bad chemistry and they will never be scheduled together. "They clash. Same kind of humor. So I keep Rickles back with Liberace where good chemistry might happen," says a "Tonight Show" producer. As they kick around the names of performers, writers, kooks, and artists, one concern is foremost in their minds: "Will Johnny relate to him?" For *that* is the secret of the show: balance and a chemistry that allows Johnny room to play.

At noon two dozen staff members meet in the producer's office to put together that night's show. They bring in chairs or lean against the walls. Few are dressed in what would be considered office attire, most look like they have made a brief detour from cutting the lawn. With clipboards in hand, they go over the show for that night, considering anything and everything that could possibly happen.

Props for skits are checked, like Art Fern's "Fork in the Road," or Ed's Smucker's topping. Rehearsal calls for musical acts are scheduled for the afternoon. Makeup calls are penciled in along with rehearsal time for the skit. Commercials, comedy bits, monologue, and karate expert, all the diverse elements of an average "Tonight Show," are efficiently assembled on mimeographed sheets, and one is given to every member of the staff, listing the lineup for that night, performers, props, commercials, musical numbers, and timing. They will all meet again at 5:00 to recheck and fill in any blank spaces caused by last minute cancellations.

Bobby Quinn, the director of the "Tonight Show," has been with NBC for over twenty-five years, most of them spent on the "Tonight Show." He was stage manager for Steve Allen and assistant director for Paar, and in between he has done lots of news directing. For the director, the "Tonight Show" is a live program. It is taped once through, ninety minutes straight. The only reason Bobby will stop the show is if there is an emergency, meaning someone has to be removed from the couch by stretcher. What would be reason enough to stop almost any other show on the air, Bobby will work around, swing with, or cover, but never stop that tape. One of the "Tonight Show's" frequently replayed segments is a Shirley Temple bit Johnny and Ed did some years ago when Shirley Temple Black was running for office. John came on-stage dressed as Miss Temple, in pigtail wig, Buster Brown shoes, and frilly tutu. What the TV viewing audience never knew was that Johnny had neglected to wear anything under the tutu, not realizing that he was on display for the first few rows in the studio. At home, it was all giggles and smiles; Quinn had covered perfectly. Then there was the time the coyote urinated on George Kirby. As much as everyone in-volved, including the coyote, wanted to stop the show, Bobby Quinn kept it rolling.

More than anyone else on the show, Bobby Quinn has to be attuned to Johnny's moods, quirks, and above all, his sense of timing; if he is not, he can ruin the show just as fast as a terrible guest. When Johnny has a dud on his hands, the director has to be ready to switch the camera to Johnny to pick up his reactions and ad libs, or the whole show will go down. Bobby has been with Johnny as long as anyone except Ed, and he is a master at anticipating lags and pauses and switching in such a way as to always keep the pace up.

It is a minor miracle the show is as polished as it is, con-sidering the rehearsal time allowed. Whoever the musical seg-ment of the show, they get an hour and fifteen minutes, from 3:15 to 4:30, to rehearse with the band. This is plenty of time if the performer is an experienced "Tonight Show" guest, and knows to bring all his own musical charts, choreography, and special props needed for the number. If not, "Doc" will have to make up some quick charts and rehearse the singer as best he can, all within that hour and fifteen minutes. Some singers, like Edie Gormet, come so well prepared they even bring their own musicians and special instruments needed for their numbers. These are the performers Bobby likes the best, leaving him time to concentrate on sets and camera shots.

Sketches are given three-quarters of an hour, from 2:30 to 3:15, no matter how long or how complex, that is all the time they get. Think of that the next time you watch the Mighty Carson Art Players ham their way through another skit. Even impossible sketches like the Western saloon brawl are given no more time. The brawl came as a result of a guest appearance by John Drury of "The Virginian," and film director Andrew McLoughlin. The sequence is reshown by Johnny from time to time, but never with the original explanation, which showed the intricate timing necessary for the illusion of total chaos. In the fight, Johnny is first grabbed by Drury and literally punched up and over the bar. He is then dragged back over the bar top and punched around some more, then back over the bar, around the saloon several times, through a window, over a table as chairs are broken over his head, and finally back out through the window once again. Actually when Johnny was thrown behind the bar or out the window, a stunt man would take his place, only to change places once again as the stunt man would be thrown over the bar again. The sequence resulted in the injury to one of the stunt men, which McLoughlin dismissed as, "part of the game. He's been there before."

The sequence is so well done that it takes a trained eye to note that Johnny is not the recipient of all the rough treatment.

The once-a-week sketches, or "five spot" fillers, are the only rehearsal Johnny does on the set, the rest of the time Bobby handles it alone. "I have nightmares," says Bobby, "about going on the air with a mystery, without a camera rehearsal, and believe me it's happened with some music groups." While the show is on the air, Bobby sits up in his control room, a nerve center that resembles the best control board at Cape Kennedy. There are banks of video screens telling him what each camera is seeing, what is happening with the commercials ready to be aired, and what is happening on the other channels. In front of the screens are row upon row of dials, switches, and levers to control every facet of the entire electronic production. Here, in a large, well-padded chair sits the director and his assistants calling the shots.

> "Ready camera two. . . . fine, now let's go in for Johnny's reaction. . . . Number three, tight on Doc. . . . Get ready to pan when Johnny crosses."
> "Thirty seconds to commercial." an assistant adds.
> "Ready number one. . . . Tight on the hands . . . no tighter . . . that's it. . . ."

and so it goes, Bobby deftly weaving the fabric together, anticipating the raised eyebrow, watching to see that the guest does not yawn on camera, cueing up the film segment brought brought by the guest, and always keeping that pace up.

For a man as concerned with being used, as Johnny is, it is a measure of his confidence and admiration in Quinn that he has no contract or signed agreement with him. Bobby Quinn has told Johnny, "As long as we two are making it together, I'll stay with you as long as you want."

During the afternoon, Ed will come down to the set for commercial rehearsal. Ed is always accompanied by the ad men and commercial pushers. He is their man—the number one second banana in all of TV, totally unflappable, always prepared and ready for any emergency. "That's my job," says Ed. "Mostly, I'm just up there in case anything unusual or extraordinary comes up."

Later Ed will get over to Freddy DeCordova's office and pick up a schedule for that night's show. He might also mention possible guests for the show, or any ideas he might have for bits, eventually wandering in to Johnny to talk about tonight's show.

Ed's vast array of other businesses keeps him from

156

full-time duty in the "Tonight Show" offices. The show, for the most part, is a complete surprise to Ed, who does not participate in its preparation except when rehearsal time is required. He does go to see Johnny just before airtime, and both of them talk themselves up for the show.

Johnny's day usually starts around 10:30. He claims not to be a chipper riser—he'll grump around the house, drinking several cups of coffee, scanning the daily papers and magazines for possible material, pulling himself together, and getting to the studio around 2 P.M. Once there Johnny changes into his working clothes. He keeps two separate sets of clothing, one for the show and another personal.

First on his daily agenda are the obligations—meeting a new sponsor, signing correspondence, and giving interviews, always with one of his press or publicity men present to clarify any statements that could cause him embarrassment if taken out of context.

If there is no sketch to rehearse, he will select the material for the monologue, go over it several times, and have it put on cue cards. He then goes over the guest list and guide-line questions and answers. If he is hungry, he will eat. One of Johnny's pet subjects is the improper eating habits of most of the world. He believes a person should eat only when hungry, which is indeed the correct way to do it. Unfortunately for most of the world, employers or family set aside a time for eating and if it is not done then, there is little chance to get another opportunity.

Everyone who works on the "Tonight Show" is quick to tell you how much they love Johnny. "Yes," they all say, "It is a grind, but Johnny is a part of us, we helped create what the public sees, and as long as Johnny does the show, we'll stay."

If the attitudes of the staff are not enough to let you know who is boss, the pictures, ranging in size from small, medium, large, all the way to giant should give some indication. It is a well-oiled, efficient machine that Johnny runs. His presence is felt rather than seen. Those who work for him know they were hired because of their abilities, not because they look busy when the boss walks through; Johnny will keep them as long as they produce. It is not necessary for him to watch them do it.

After reviewing his monologue or special bits for that night's show, Johnny, accompanied by Freddy DeCordova, will head for his make-up room, where they will go over parts of the show while Johnny's make-up man applies the orange pancake to his face and hands.

Nearby is the guest's make-up room, complete with huge swiveling barber chairs and make-up people so immaculately manicured and dressed one might wonder who is going to be on the show. After receiving their orange masks (white for women), the guests wait backstage in the Green Room.

The Green Room is literally that. It exists in some form in every professional theater. In a sleazy theater the room is painted green and the paint is usually peeling; at the "Tonight Show" it is green fabric wall coverings so permeated with the stench of fear, one actor describes the smell "like an old hat." The Green Room has many euphemisms: the Snake Pit, the Anxiety Room, or as Joan Rivers calls it, "Torture Terrace."

Here the guests assemble with their respective agents, publishers, and personal managers. Some bring their own make-up specialists and hairdressers. Guests are easy to spot; they are the ones not dressed in shiny suits. All the special quirks and special bits of preparation performers use to calm themselves down or get their energy up are on open display here. The talent coordinators soothe and reassure their particular guests, offering a nip from the Green Room bar if it is desired. There is vodka, scotch, or coffee. No ice here, no one kids himself, this is no social drink. The talent coordinators watch carefully to see that no one gets too many, but sometimes they do not watch carefully enough.

There is a large color video monitor in the room so guests can watch the show. Most do, or talk to their agents; no one talks to anyone they did not bring with them.

As the studio audience lines up to take their seats, a production assistant will go down the line with instructions for that night's show.

"All right. Tonight we play stump the band. Has anyone

got some crazy songs for Doc and the band?" intones the assistant, projecting enough for everyone to hear. Hands fly up as housewives from Kenosha and insurance salesmen from Spokane blurt out lyrics raw enough to make a drill seargeant wince. Several more acceptable songs will be selected and those people will be seated on the aisle. Next the production assistant will go down the line looking for "beautiful people," the good looking women will then get seats in the first several rows, where the camera can pick them up when it pans. When the show was in New York, the audience would assemble upstairs in Rockefeller Center and then make the trip to the studio below in an elevator, seventeen at a time. Now in their new home at the NBC studios in Burbank, the process is much simpler—they merely walk in.

The first thing the audience will notice is the temperature. It is cold. The studio is kept cold because a cold tense audience will laugh more. "Christ, when Paar was here," says ex-head writer Walter Kempley, "you could store meat down there."

The band will begin to filter on, fidgeting with their instruments until Doc comes flamboyantly onstage from a rehearsal room just off the studio. He and the band do several numbers, Doc clowning it up a bit and then out comes "Big Ed." Ed does the audience warm-up, a form of comedy renowned as the worst. It is not really Ed's fault; he is not the star of the show and he knows it. Besides, he cannot do anything in the warm-up that might step on part of Johnny's monologue and that effectively rules out any reference to current events or any of the established "Tonight Show" laugh-getters. Ed then explains the show to the audience, pointing out the applause signs and the TV monitors, telling the, ". . . so if you're here on a Ha-Ha convention with someone you shouldn't be with, duck when the camera comes your way."

It is a joke, but NBC has found it wise to warn people that NBC is not legally liable, since candid shots have gotten the show in trouble with irate audience members in the past.

Finally, the time is at hand. Ed goes to his stand-up mike to the left of the stage and delivers the introduction which has become better know than "Gentlemen start your engines"; "Play ball!"; or possibly even "Friends, Romans, and countrymen . . ."

"And now . . . here's Johnny!"

The curtains part and out he comes: the familiar walk, the hands touching his cufflinks, then his face and into his pockets, the smile. We know it all, we have seen it six nights a week for thirteen years, and we are going to watch it again tonight and again tomorrow.

> "I see Ed's back. He wasn't with us last night, he had to go to the hospital to have his hands checked. . . . Someone stepped on them on his way home."

The audience howls. The cue card boys move the monologue in front, just out of camera view. Freddy nods approvingly as the audience swings with Johnny's routine. He turns to see Doc.

> "You look like a receptionist for Gay Liberation."

Up in the director's booth, Bobby Quinn is moving for a long shot of Doc, then as Doc turns, "Number two . . . tight shot on the back of the vest."

Half way through Johnny hits a "valley."

> "Whew! Well, they can't all be gems. . . . This audience isn't as bad as the one we had last night."

"How bad was it?" comes the cry from the back of the audience. (We all know the routines.)

> "It was so bad, there was a woman in the first row knitting a noose."

Back in the Green Room the waiting starlet lights another cigarette, forgetting she already has three burning. Vodka is poured to the sound of pill cases closing, "Just one Vallium to even me out."

"Now there's an example of one of the oldest rules of comedy. . . . Never tell three polar bear jokes in succession."

"Where is that written?" asks Ed.

The show is rolling. Johnny, using his writer's material as a springboard, has the audience with him now. Carl Reiner once said of Jack Benny, "you never felt embarrassed for him. If the material didn't work, so what?" Johnny generates much the same feeling. He's never going to make us squirm. We can relax with him.

"Say, we really have a great show for you tonight. . . . It's coming on right after this one. . . . But seriously folks . . ."

The band lifts their instruments. Johnny takes a swing with his imaginary golf club. Bobby Quinn cuts to a commercial, and Johnny heads for the desk along with Ed. When we return, it is for a rundown of the propositions on the ballot in the upcoming California primary election. Johnny reads a random sampling.

"It's interesting how a paper like the *L.A. Times* will have everything you could ever want to know about the election propositions." hams Ed.

"Not everything Moose Breath. I have here some propositions that didn't make it to the ballot."

This is the "Five Spot" and Johnny's propositions are not going over well with the studio audience. Ed is on the floor as Johnny struggles with the material. The audience does not have the vaguest idea of what Ed is laughing about. At home we know and laugh with Ed.

The first guest comes on and does his bit, Johnny laughing spontaneously at stories he already knows. The guest told him the same story the last time he was on, and even if he had not, Johnny heard it when he was working for WOW in Omaha. Johnny reacts beautifully, checking his producer, Freddy DeCordova, every minute or two to make sure he is playing it right.

161

DeCordova sits as close as possible while not getting under the wheels of the giant color cameras, goading, laughing, reacting to Johnny's every move or inflection. At times it seems they play to each other and not the guest. On station breaks, Freddy will come up to the desk, Johnny usually sits tapping a pencil; seldom does he talk to the guest. Whatever the reason, it is smart production not to talk; better the guest should do it for the camera than over a dead microphone. It is for this reason that Johnny never talks to guests before they appear. Occasionally he will poke his head into the Green Room and say a general hello, but never anything more than that. This practice has aggravated many guests who do not understand, without the cameras Johnny would never talk to them at all. It is a show and there is nothing else on Johnny's mind.

Every guest does his bit, then slips the plugs in—plugs for upcoming theatrical events, movies, plays, TV specials, etc. These are fine with Johnny, as are plugs for charity, books, or records. What is not OK are plugs for products not advertised on the "Tonight Show." There is no quicker way to bring on a commercial than with an improper plug. Once Zsa Zsa Gabor went on at such length about her new line of cosmetics that Bobby Quinn cut her off and punched in a commercial for a competing cosmetic line.

The best approach is when the guest allows Johnny to do the plug. If the guest can hang in there long enough, Johnny will usually give the guest an excellent mention, which means much more to the viewing public than the guest tooting his own horn. Most, however, can never seem to wait, suspecting that Johnny does not know why they are there.

After allowing three and a half minutes for the guests, Johnny tells us who the next night's guests will be and closes the show with a brief recap of the guest's plugs, thanks them all for coming, and says goodnight, coming from behind the desk to shake hands while the credits are rolled.

After the show John will go back to his office and have a Coke or a bottle of Michelob beer and unwind by himself. He cleans up, changes into his own clothes, and heads for home—the same as anyone else who has finished his work for the day.

The show is over, but it has yet to be broadcast. All that remains of the efforts of over a hundred people is a tin of video tape roughly the size of an LP record, but several inches thick. After it has been respooled and broadcast it will be rewound, put back in the tin, and placed on a shelf with a hundred other tapes. Freddy DeCordova will review last week's tapes and decide which, if any, should be kept for rebroadcast, or what segments might work well for the once a year anniversary show. Each tape costs $350 and can be erased and re-used fifty times. Over 90 percent of the "Tonight Show" tapes are erased and re-used, only a hundred are kept for Saturday night replays and occasional emergencies.

The "Tonight Show" continues to run smoothly with no letdown in quality, which usually is not the case with television shows once they have become popular and command a habit audience. This is because of the concern of one man—Johnny Carson. Sloppiness, and haphazard work habits are not a part of his character and they are not a part of his show either. He stays away from most aspects of production, but there is nothing that happens with his show that he does not know about, that he does not OK or nix. The lessons CBS taught him on that first "Johnny Carson Show" were learned well. Control is everything, and Johnny controls everything. Like his tight suitcase, he runs a tight ship.

Chapter Nine

With the exception of Johnny's three sons, no one has been with him longer than Ed McMahon. It is even doubtful that his sons have spent as much time as Ed with Johnny. As with any relationship, there have been tensions, riffs, and near splits between the two, but each always recognizes in time the near-perfect complementary nature of their performance together and pulls back from the edge. Because Johnny is the absolute boss, Ed has done most of the pulling back, but Johnny is aware of Ed's territorial prerogatives and is careful not to tread where he does not belong.

Everyone always marvels at the way Johnny can pull a dying comedy routine out of the fire, which indeed he can. But a large measure of his success working around bad material on the "Tonight Show" has been, at least in part, because of his ability to play to Ed when the studio audience has rejected him. Ed, more than the studio audience, resembles the intelligence and sophistication of the viewing public. Johnny has always said about Ed, "I sincerely believe he thinks I'm funny, and that's a big help." When Ed laughs there is no mistaking it for a giggle or a smirk. The man *laughs*, so much so that at times he has been criticized for it. It must be genuine; if it is not, he deserves an Emmy every year for the most convincing acting on television.

Ed did not fall into his role because he fell short of a quest for the top. He started out to be a second banana, his early radio idol being Paul Douglas, the second banana for Fred Waring. Says Ed of Paul, "I always admired him. He sounded like he was talking to you and not just the air."

Being number two might have induced Ed to try harder, though there is no time in Ed's life when he was not trying. All the effort has made Ed second only to Johnny on the show. Off the show, Ed's many business interests have made him a wealthy man, surpassed by Johnny only in recent years. By any yardstick, Ed is a big man. One wonders how he ever manages to cram six-feet four-inches and 230 plus pounds into the cockpits of the airplanes he flies for the marines as a reserve lieutenant colonel.

An only child born in Detroit in 1923, Ed's father left the plumbing business to become an interlocutor, a man who introduces the performers and acts as a straight man in a minstrel show. As they say, the apple does not fall that far. The senior McMahon later moved from job to job, along the way acting as fund raiser for clubs and charities and moving the family to Bayonne, New Jersey, Olney, Pennsylvania, and Lowell, Massachusetts. By the time Ed had reached the age of seventeen, he had been in fifteen different schools—good training for a man who would spend the rest of his life trying to cope with constantly changing situations.

At the age of fifteen, Ed got his first break as a barker in a local carnival in Mexico, Maine, moving from there to the state fair in Schaghticoke, New York, as second banana to "The Best Bingo Caller in the World." When the number one man got "sick," Ed went on in his place as "the Second-Best Bingo Caller in the World." A career was launched.

As with Johnny, Ed's first love was radio. Spurred on by his early admiration of Paul Douglas, he practiced radio commercials by cueing up the family's old RCA wind-up victrola and played radio by reading the ads out of *Time* magazine. All the practice paid off when he got to college. At Boston University, he played football and earned extra money as a sportscaster, weatherman, and D.J. on WLLH in Lowell, Massachusetts. The man he replaced was Ray Goulding, who was later known in the world for his part in the Bob and Ray team. (Incidentally, it was Bob and Ray who were the forerunners of TV commercial comedy with their act as Bert and Harry Piel.)

World War II cut Ed's stay at Boston College short. Ed

enlisted in the marines, where he became a fighter pilot and spent the war stateside as an instructor. While stationed in Jacksonville, Florida, he met and married a southern belle, Alice Farrell.

After the war, Ed applied to Catholic University in Washington, D.C., under the GI bill and was accepted. However, he had no money to make the move from Florida so he went to Atlantic City and hustled fountain pens on the boardwalk. It was the beginning of a love affair, for many summers after that Ed returned to the boardwalk to sell one thing or another. His specialty was the vegetable slicer. If you have never been to Atlantic City and watched these men work, you've been missing a good show. Not only is it fun, but as Ed puts it, "Have you ever seen one of those guys work slicing potatoes?" When talking about these men, Ed uses tones normally reserved for luminaries of the highest order. "That's as far as you can go selling people what they don't need." Without a moment's hesitation, it all floods back. There he is atop his soap box, the counter before him spread with fruits and vegetables ready for slicing. He gathers the crowd around, urging them to get ever closer, whetting the appetite. Eagerly they wait, knowing they are about to see a bona fide miracle of modern man. It is called "turning the tip." Whether it is soft sell on TV or out there in the open air of the boardwalk, there is no one in the world better at "turning the tip" than Ed McMahon.

> "Folks, I'm gonna show you the Morris Metric Slicer. Two dollars is the price on the box, but forget the two dollars. I'm talking about one dollar, and I'm throwing in the onion slicer and the juice extractor."

Today Ed no longer goes to Atlantic City; he "turns the tip" on a national scale.

Once enrolled at Catholic U., Ed had to find a way to support his family. He and another student—who later went on to become a Baptist minister—started a dry cleaning business. They operated out of the back of Ed's car. The service must have been good because they soon found business

166

booming. Estimates of his earnings while in college range as high as $600 a week. Always a hustler, there has never been a time when Ed was involved in only one thing at a time. Ed graduated from Catholic U. with a degree in speech and drama, and today he heads their alumni association. Several years ago the university called on Ed to put together an all-star show to raise money for the school. For Ed it was no problem; he just called his drinking buddies and gathered together enough all-stars to make the Academy Awards envious.

Before starting his career in earnest, the Korean War broke out. Ed was called back, and this time not as an instructor. He was sent to Korea for combat duty, where he flew eighty-five missions as an artillery observer (the guy who flies the little piper cub into a fire zone and then radios back telling the guys shooting the guns what they have hit and where the next rounds should go). He won six air medals.

Ed's first introduction to television was at station WCAU-TV, Philadelphia, where he remains something of a legend to this day. In Philadelphia he was known as Mr. Television since he had appeared on as many as thirteen shows simultaneously. It was during this time that Ed got the reputation for being a heavy drinker; since then, his drinking habits have been considerably curtailed.

Ed left Philadelphia to take the job with Johnny as announcer on "Who Do You Trust," keeping his family in Philadelphia and commuting daily to the show. Right from the start, he and John hit it off well, on camera as well as off. Ed showed Johnny Carson from Norfolk, Nebraska, what most Irishmen know about bars before they are out of the crib. During those years and on into the early years of the "Tonight Show," he and Ed were frequent visitors to most of New York's clubs. It was at this time that Johnny found he had a tendency to get "hostile," as he puts it, when drinking. Once, while in the exclusive New York restaurant Voisin, Jacqueline Susann reputedly threw a drink in his face when John refused to leave after making nuisance of himself.

She said of him later, "A tremendous performer, but not one of my favorite people."

167

That was not the last Jacqueline was to hear of Johnny or the "Tonight Show." Later, Truman Capote, while on the show one night, accused her of an assortment of poor writing habits, ending with, ". . . I mean, after all, she looks just like a truck driver in drag." That comment brought a lawsuit.

When Johnny left "Who Do You Trust" he took two people with him: producer Art Stark and Ed. Ed soon gained the reputation for being one of the best straight men in the business. "I'm a catcher," says Ed, *He's* the guy who does the throwing." Those early years were still a time for testing; the performance relationship between Ed and Johnny had not yet defined its boundaries, and many was the time Ed walked on Johnny's laughs.

With the move to Rockefeller Center, Ed was assigned to take Charlie Weaver's place at Hurley's bar, and there was joking about Hurley's, which soon became ritualized in Johnny's monologue as the Ed drinking stories. When asked about the constant joking about his drinking, Ed says, "It's all in fun. It helps the show and it isn't bad once you get used to it." But you can tell that sometimes the teasing is not welcome. "Besides . . . he's the boss," Ed adds.

"Ed was picked up by the Los Angeles cops last night and got 100 percent on the breath test. . . . He's going to try for his post-graduate degree just as soon as they give him his license back."

During Johnny's feud with NBC, Ed became the scapegoat. "When Johnny refused to do the first fifteen minutes, it fell to Skitch and myself to do them," Ed explains. "I didn't want to do the first fifteen minutes either. I wasn't being paid any extra money, and the problem was that we couldn't step on Johnny's monologue. We couldn't talk about anything he might be going to say—nothing in the newspapers, nothing topical. If we'd just been in California, I couldn't even say, 'Well, here we are back in New York.'"

The first fifteen is much different from the warm-up. Only a couple of hundred people in the studio see the warm-up. The first fifteen minutes go out to most of the country; it is no place to bomb. "We were stuck with being bland and neutral. And inadvertently, I did stumble in on Johnny's area," Ed says of that time.

Johnny raised the roof, and Ed tried a power play of his own. He refused to do the first fifteen minutes also. "I took a stand," recalls Ed, "We had a confrontation, out of which it was decided that I would do the first fifteen." The boundaries were beginning to be marked more plainly.

As always, Ed soon had his finger in several more pies. He had a daily radio program on NBC called "Monitor," and for a while a day-time television quiz show, "Snap Judgment." But Ed's real bread and butter was still the "Tonight Show," and this was the springboard he would use to so many other endeavors. Ed explains, "John knows I won't throw him anything too hot to handle. It's like a cat with a ball—never hit it so far that you can't get it back."

But in the early spring of 1965, Ed almost hit it too far. Insiders say that it went so far that Johnny said one night, "I don't want him back on the show tomorrow night!"

At that point, Johnny was not so secure and he did not feel he could stand the competition from Ed. Johnny thought Ed was getting too many laughs. He was also displeased with Ed's constant riding of Skitch Henderson, then a close friend of John's. Ed was simply getting too strong, and it all came to a head with the mosquito incident. Johnny was telling how mosquitoes only go for the really passionate people. Ed instinctively slapped his arm, thereby stepping on Johnny's laugh. That was as close as they ever came to splitting. Ed said he thought his spokesman position with Budweiser saved him. "I apologized for that one. I couldn't help myself. Playing second banana with him causes some problems. You can't take away from the star. What makes a good second banana is a guy who can walk that tightrope without falling off." The boundaries were now being marked in bold lines. Ed was almost through testing; Johnny had told him where he thought his position should be. Now it was up to Ed to either be satisfied with it or risk a permanent parting.

Ed went through a period of saying very little on the show.

When asked how he does it, a "Tonight Show" staff member put it this way, "Look, when you get into that extra-income bracket, you just hide your feelings."

Ed hid them well and now is as big as anyone in television, except Johnny, of course. It is difficult to explain exactly what Ed does on the show, and Ed was at great pains to explain it to his young son. With no acceptable answer coming, his son asked, "Do you dig in the sand in New York?"

Ed thought about it a moment then nodded, "Yeah. That's pretty much what I do."

Ed now leaves the show to Johnny, helping him out of a jam when he needs it. Otherwise he moves down the couch as each new guest pushes him wordlessly farther from the desk. The "Tonight Show" takes roughly five hours out of Ed's day, leaving him plenty of time for the rest of his businesses. There are many. Unicorn Creations produces greeting cards and pop-art paper products. Then there is Del-Sol, a film production and graphic arts company. Among Del-Sol's many credits is the design for the Vatican exhibit at the 1964 New York World's Fair. They also produce documentaries and titles for motion pictures. Delphi Productions is a talent agency and Parthenon Productions pays his secretaries salary, owns his car, and pays for Ed's maid. Another of Ed's companies is Corinthian Productions, which, at the present time, does nothing. His business interests range from the manufacture of shopping bags to film companies, talent agencies, drive-in stores and much more. But Ed has become a celebrity in his own right. He is able to handle contact with people more easily than John. It seems there is no one who does not know Ed from somewhere, and this has always been the case.

Keeping track of Ed's extra-curricular activities would take one full-time person. There is never a week that does not find Ed off somewhere. If it is not a charity function, it is an appearance for Budweiser, which handsomely rewards him for being their spokesman.

He has been the voice of General Motors and the radio spokesman for Breck shampoo. Always on a new diet, several

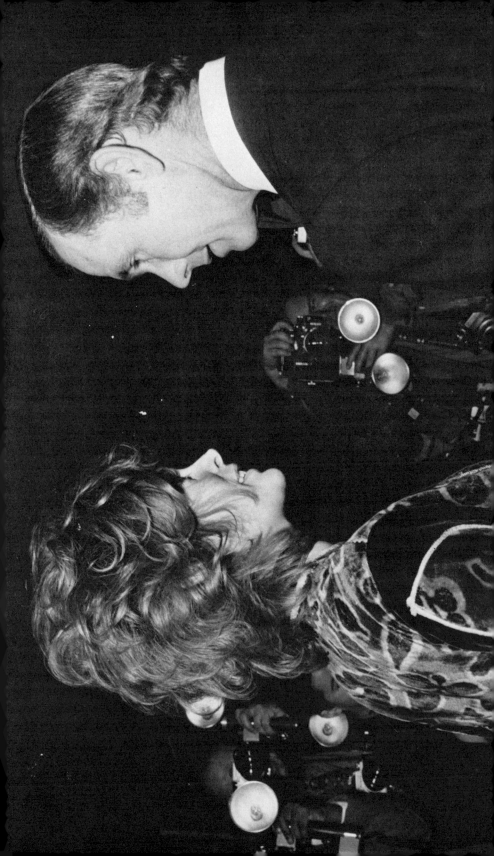

years ago a fad diet book hit the market pitched by none other than Ed himself.

Ed has made several movies, and replaced Alan King on Broadway in *The Impossible Years* for a week.

Does Ed ever stop? No. Recently, he followed Johnny's lead and hit the night club trail with an act of his own. Ed starts the act out with his pitch for the Morris Metric Slicer and then goes to drunk stories and barroom songs. On his opening night Ed did something he had never done before—he took off part of his thumb in the Morris Metric Slicer. The event hit most of the newspapers, but at the time, Johnny was on vacation and no one had told him about it. Returning, he noticed Ed's heavily bandaged thumb and asked him about it. As the story was told to Johnny for the first time on the air, he laughed so hard that the tears began to roll down his face and his chair went back from the desk. This was obviously something he had fantasized about many times before.

In early 1972 the "Tonight Show" moved permanently to Los Angeles. Ed went with the show, leaving his wife Alice behind. On February 22, 1972, Alice charged Ed with abandonment and asked for $60,000 a year in support and alimony. Ed had to pay the $60,00, $50,000 of which went to Alice and $10,000 to her lawyer.

Ed has always run with a different crowd than Johnny. His connections with powerful people like Sinatra, many feel, saved him from big trouble with the Teamsters. Ed and several associates had borrowed a few million dollars from Nick Torzeski. Through some slick bookkeeping, Nick had apparently loaned Ed the money from Teamster accounts. The trouble developed when Ed's operation diverted portions of the money from the hotels it was to be used for to an abortive motion picture. When the picture did not work out and Nick wanted his money back, things got a little sticky, some saying Nick had gone so far as to threaten Ed with a contract. The full details of the incident have never been revealed, but apparently Ed's friends managed to pull him through it all right.

Now living on the West Coast with the "Tonight Show,"

Ed is still doing what he does best—walking that tightrope without falling. He has wavered many times, but the big man has never fallen.

Johnny is acknowledged as the best at what he does, and Ed gets the same grades for what he does. The *third* star of the show is musical director, Carl "Doc" Severnson, who draws little debate about his competence. Doc plays the trumpet and acts as musical director of the greatest band in the world. With few exceptions, every singer or musical performer on the "Tonight Show" will finish their number, cross to the chair next to Johnny, and say something like, "Thanks fellas. Johnny, I have to tell you, that is the finest group of musicians I have ever worked with." If the performer brings his own charts, he is amazed to hear the music played just as he had wanted it. If he does not bring his own music, Doc and Tommy Newsome throw together an arrangement, on the spot, that the performer would have to pay hundreds or thousands of dollars for somewhere else under different circumstances.

There has been no poll of the finest trumpet players published anywhere in the last five years that does not include Doc's name. Like almost everything else about the show, Doc is one of the Biggest and the Best.

With his unique cross between "hip" and country/western accents Doc says, "I was born in Arlington, Oregon, the year Lindy flew the ocean and the Babe hit sixty homers." The nickname "Doc" is actually short for "Little Doc." His father was a dentist in Arlington and was known as "Big Doc."

Doc first took up the trumpet when he was seven years old. Always a fast learner and incessant practicer, he was playing in the Arlington High School orchestra three weeks later.

When he finished high school, Doc hit the road, playing with big bands like Benny Goodman and Tommy Dorsey, eventually finding a seat in the NBC studio orchestra, where he worked his way up to the position he now holds.

Al Klink, who for years played sax next to Doc in the NBC orchestra, says, "Doc's the warming-upest trumpet player I ever saw. He spends every spare minute practicing in a little dressing room near the studio. Doc sometimes practices till two or three in the morning."

Some say this is because he is so insecure. No so, say many members of the band. They'll tell you that Doc plays some of the hardest trumpet music in the business and he *has* to keep up his lip.

Today Doc lives in California with the rest of the "Tonight Show" staff, and like Johnny and Ed, he left his wife on the East Coast.

Doc also hits the night club and casino circuit with his own show entitled The Now Generation Brass, a big band heavy brass sound with just enough rock thrown in to appeal to everyone. Good looking, well-built, young women do the vocal line to accompany Doc's heady trumpet runs. The costumes are vintage Doc—lots of sequins, wild colors, and insane hand-painted, skin-tight outfits that Johnny "wouldn't wear to Liberace's wake."

Taken as a whole, the "Tonight Show" is the best of its kind. Even when broken down to its individual elements, it is difficult to find a weak link. They are all good, they know it, and they are paid for it.

Chapter Ten

After all the publicity from his walkout had died down, John settled down to the routine of the show once again. His new producer was Stan Irwin, the man responsible for getting Johnny $40,000 a week for his Las Vegas act. Irwin is an ex-writer, comic, and former vice-president and executive producer of the Sahara Nevada Corporation. He has claimed to be the nation's biggest booker of talent, exceeding $10,000,000 a year in gross payments.

The "Tonight Show" began to have a bit more variety because of one of the clauses in John's new contract that stopped NBC from forcing him to accept as guests every NBC "star" promoting a new show or trying to punch some life into an already dead series. The "Tonight Show" had become a litter basket for NBC and John now put an end to it.

He and Joanne were in the process of buying up adjoining apartments in their building in United Nations Plaza, breaking down walls to make a mini-compound high above Manhattan. Joanne handled all the interior design herself, building the decor around the theme of Johnny Carson. "It's a house built for privacy." said Joanne. She and Johnny have spent many hours there, seldom going out except for an occasional trip to "safe" restaurants like Peter's Backyard.

The couple never had any children of their own; Johnny had complete custody of his three sons when they were not in boarding school. Asked if she wanted a child, Joanne replied, "I've got one. Me. One child in the family is enough."

Other than work, Johnny seldom ventured from the compound, preferring to spend the time with his wife. After living so closely with the man, Joanne is genuinely baffled by questions of Johnny's true character, "What you see on that screen is really Johnny. That's what he's really like. It happens to be true—he is a loner—people just don't understand." So John stayed safe and secure in his $178,000 cooperative compound.

When he did venture out, it always seemed as if something happened to confirm all his fears about being used. In June of 1967 John won a restraining order to keep his picture out of a brochure for the Drake Institute of Hypnosis, a St. Louis-based school. The picture in question showed David Drake and Johnny seated on a couch. It was taken without John's knowledge while on a visit to St. Louis. Opposite the picture in the brochure were testimonials from several people claiming all kinds of rewards—monetary, spiritual, and otherwise—resulting from courses taken at the Drake Institute of Hypnosis. The caption under the photo read: "David Drake and Johnny Carson at an NBC party." In addition to the restraining order, John also sued for $300,000 in damages.

With ABC already committed to late-night talk shows, and several syndicated shows running well, it began to look like the Promised Land to programming executives, who would soon swamp the viewers with a sea of talk. The only thing stopping them were indications that success might not be guaranteed. One sign was the premiere of Bill Dana's variety talk show out of Las Vegas, which sponsored a truly all-star lineup. The overnight ratings came in and the show placed fifth, behind Merv, Joey, and Johnny, but the real surprise that night was CBS's late movie, *The Incredible Shrinking Man,* an admitted grade B movie that drew an astounding 26 percent, topping everything else on the air. Who knows for sure what the public wants. An indication came the next night when Johnny was safely back on top.

The "Tonight Show" continued with the same light, easy entertainment as before. The chance for truly outrageous situations was cut to a minimum, but they happened all the same. Ed Ames, Mingo the Indian in the Daniel Boone TV series, showed John how to throw a tomahawk. The target was a crudely painted outline of a man on a large oak board. Ed took aim and let the tomahawk fly, hitting the outline squarely in the crotch. It was a classic moment for television bloopers, and Johnny reshows the segment once a year. Though most of us have seen it ten times, that segment alone makes his anniversary show worth watching.

It was moments like these that made the "Tonight Show" the most talked about show on the air. People mentioned it as frequently as they used to talk of the old dramatic series "Playhouse 90" and "Studio One."

Aware of the impact the show was having, NBC commissioned several studies to see just who was watching and why. Their studies revealed the bulk of the audience to be upper- and middle-income families with a better than average education. Blue collar workers, it was found, go to bed too early. People are in and out viewers also, i.e., they watch the segments of the show that interest them and leave the room for the others.

The most interesting aspect of the studies was summed up in a new word "closure" —meaning people watching a show automatically filling in the missing element. We all know the policeman we see in black and white is in reality dressed in blue. We do not think about it; we just know it. When viewers look at Carson, the researchers found, the missing element they filled in was themselves—they felt as if *they* were talking to Tony Randall instead of Johnny.

When first taking over the "Tonight Show," Johnny had said, "If I get a two-week vacation, I'll be damned if I'm going to Las Vegas. I'll take my kids and go out to Colorado." Johnny was getting more than two week's vacation, and he was spending most of it in Las Vegas, where he had become one of the biggest headliners. He has always said how much he liked working with a live audience and being able to work without the restrictions placed on him by the network and the sponsors. His nightclub routine is never done on TV as John believes it is improper to give the television viewers what others have to pay to see.

The act consists of a bit of everything, most of which could not be done on television. After a complete physical checkup at the Mayo Clinic, John built a whole segment of the act around this experience. "They give you a stem to stern checkup, especially stern. . . . The nurse gives me a little jelly jar and I dry up like the Mojave Desert. . . . The last time I had castor oil I was eight years old and believe me, it works just the same." There is a lot of tearing at television commercials and plenty of breast jokes: "Women don't like topless shows, they say to their husbands, 'You'd get sick if you had to look at that all day.' But Carlo Ponti hasn't had a sick day in his life."

He also has used his nightclub act to hit people he felt it improper to hit on television. When columnist Dorothy Kilgallen tried to start another feud with Carson, in much the same way she had with Paar, Johnny ignored her charges of his improper conduct during Lyndon Johnson's inaugural, choosing to let her have it in his club act where no one could stop him." Dorothy Kilgallen is the only woman I wouldn't mind my wife catching me with. . . . I don't know why she took such umbrage at my comments on birth control, she's such a living argument for it." The point was made. Unlike the overemotional Paar, Johnny got *his* mileage out of the feud and Kilgallen got nothing.

Some measure of his soaring popularity was the *New York Post*'s two-column spread on the theft of his NBC limousine containing eight brand new turtleneck sweaters and a pair of Joanne's thigh-high boots.

Despite his aversion to controversial guests, Johnny decided to have New Orleans District Attorney Jim Garrison on to talk of his "conclusive" new evidence concerning the Kennedy assassination. The show got quite a build-up and drew a huge audience, but Garrison's revelations seemed to be another set of unexplained coincidences and no hard facts. The debate rages today, but not on the "Tonight Show." Johnny had given air time to the most controversial argument in America. There could not have been a more guaranteed controversial guest at that time; yet Shecky Green on an off night had more to say than Garrison. John was more convinced than ever, controversy just was not his cup of tea.

What was his cup of tea were Plimptonesque stunts, such

177

as his first parachute jump. On his first time out John chose, rather than a static line jump in which the chute opens automatically, a 10,000-foot free fall before opening his parachute. Then he drove Andy Granatelli's outlawed turbine racing car around the Indianapolis speedway at speeds over 170 miles an hour. There was no keeping John in the studio. Every opportunity found him off on another crazy escapade, some of them very dangerous. He flew in a hot air balloon, and took a sky ride, hanging from a huge kite towed by a racing speed boat.

It was all fun and games until NBC decided to test Johnny's new contract. "Just this week I found that somebody at NBC sold a football game for Monday night and they want me to cut down my show. I won't do the show any night, anymore, unless it starts at 11:30," John told them.

This was in the late summer of 1968. The National Football League had decided to test viewer support of nighttime football during the week. NBC had told John to tape a full ninety-minute show, and then they would decide how much of the show to televise. An NBC executive rationalized it by saying, "It's not at all unusual for a show to be cancelled if a sporting event runs too long."

Possibly, but that was not the way John saw it. "Unless my program starts at 11:30 I do not plan to do a show. It is the only recourse I have to protect my show. Anything is habit. If the show does not go on at the scheduled time, of course it is detrimental to the show. Pretty soon people won't know if we're there or not."

NBC still maintained that John was taking an unreasonable stand and went ahead with plans for the football game.

"It's not fair to treat my show like a late-night filler. It is the biggest money-maker they have, and if they start moving it around, they are jeopardizing my career and also a contractual obligation."

No sooner were the words "contractual obligation" out of John's mouth than his lawyers were at NBC's door to "show them the facts of life" concerning their contract with John. The show was now on the other foot. The lawyers read the contract chapter and verse, calling their attention to Johnny's right to approve any variety type show put on in place of the "Tonight Show," his right to refuse to run a tape made earlier than the air date, and his right to refuse any guest host. Legitimately arguing that he runs the risk of losing his "habit" audience, NBC finally concurred and, rather than run an old movie, went black after the football game.

John's lawyers were not through. They looked at the upcoming schedule and found NBC had planned an extra long movie that would also cut into the "Tonight Show." The air date was the anniversary of the show.

NBC assured John that they would not run the movie then.

"What about the future?" the lawyers wanted to know.

NBC promised to run any movies that might possibly cut into the "Tonight Show" on Saturdays from now on.

John's sexual references are usually quite mild compared to what is broadcast on the soap operas during the day, but in late 1967 NBC felt one of his skits should be censored and with John's consent, they cut a couple of lines. Later NBC decided four more lines should be cut before air time. John told them to scrap the entire episode rather than to air it hacked to pieces. The next night Johnny came on and explained the deletion of the night before. Then, to rub salt in the wound of NBC, he showed how network "bleeps" can often be worse than the original line.

"Jack and Jill went up the hill to ————."
"Little Miss Muffet sat on her ————."

At Christmas that year NBC came to Johnny's PR man, Al Husted, and asked him for a suggestion on what to get Johnny for a present. Al gave it some serious thought and came up with an idea for a clock from Tiffany's. The clock would be impressive, explained Husted, ". . . and where the numerals are eleven and twelve o'clock, why don't we replace them with a special inset, eleven-thirty in diamonds or something."

The network executives thought that was just great until they asked Al the price. It was $2300. "Oh," was the stunned reply, "what we really had in mind was something around $100."

This was the capstone. At last Johnny realized that although he might be the most successful man in the world running the "Tonight Show," he was losing the war with NBC. He simply did not have the super-business savvy required of a man in his position. He was winning the little battles along the way, but NBC was not about to stop nipping at his heels until he fell. He was dealing with a giant and now needed a giant in his corner. He was making a huge salary by any layman's standards, but not really that much by the standards of the industry.

He turned to one of his neighbors in his co-op, Sonny Werblin, former owner of the New York Jets and ex-financial tycoon of MCA, the giant talent agency. Johnny and Joanne flew to Florida to ask for Sonny's help. Joanne and Mrs. Werblin already were friends from their contact in the building and this weighed heavily in John's favor.

Sonny said he would take John on, he would be one of three show business clients Sonny advised, the others being Joe Namath and Jimmy Brown. Sonny refuses to talk of the state of John's business affairs before he became involved. He acknowledges their existence by saying, "I think that's why I'm in the picture."

First, Sonny formed a corporation with him and John as sole partners, eliminating all the old lawyers and agents. The corporate name of Raritan was chosen in honor of Sonny's alma mater Rutgers, which is situated on the banks of the Raritan River. The new corporation would take over the production of the "Tonight Show" from NBC. It would also negotiate all the new contracts, with a heavy emphasis on deferred payment to cut into the tremendous tax burden Johnny was carrying in the belief that taxpayers should not resort to tax dodges. Raritan would also begin production of specials and pilots for NBC. The "Sun City Scandals" special was one of these. They would also look for outside income for Johnny, and not the type that required him to pose with a Saint Bernard for a vodka ad, which he had done just a year before.

The instant the shutter snapped, "I kind of regretted doing it," said John.

Some of the investments would turn into multi-million dollar properties, others would be better forgotten. One of those better forgotten was John's entrance into the fast-food craze. The press luncheon to herald the opening of Johnny's American Inn, Inc. found John fighting hard to stay awake as one of the lawyers for a food company droned on in an endless speech. As the lawyer was concluding with a tribute to an absent executive, John did exactly what he would do with a guest this dull on the "Tonight Show": he chimed in just as the lawyer was getting to the part about "a man of great integrity, vision and foresight . . ."

"And he couldn't make it today," piped John, "because he's involved in a paternity suit."

As ever, the audience loved it. The executives did not.

The menu for Johnny's American Inns featured such items as The Big Bird of Paradise fried chicken plate, Here's Johnny cole slaw, and the HOW BIG IS IT? cheeseburger.

Johnny got another trip to Washington out of it all. This time he appeared before a senate committee investigating franchise operations. Johnny, who owns 15 percent of American Inns, was a bit peeved, and told the senate committee, "I am a little resentful of the attitude here that a performer has no knowledge of business."

Sonny now sorted the legitimate business propositions from the money-making schemes. Carson has never had to look farther than his daily mail for money-making schemes. The pitch usually starts by asking for just a little bit up front, say $250,000. Most common offers are for chinchilla farms, diamond mines, and new game shows. One hopeful wanted to raise the *Andrea Doria* if John went for the seed money. The salvager was offering to rename her the *S.S. Johnny Carson*.

Sonny sent Johnny out to the heartland with his nightclub act, playing such caverns as the Lubbock auditorium in Lubbock, Texas, then up to Wisconsin where he drew $60,000 in one night. For one performance in Minneapolis, John pulled in $75,000. John's cut of all this money was 60 percent.

JOHNNY CARSON

Johnny had been approached by a number of clothing manufacturers to lend his name to a line of their clothes. He had always turned down the offers, never believing the manufacturers would do anything but use his name and then drop him.

Hart, Schaffner and Marx had had their eye on producing another line of clothes that would not compete with their Grade 4, first-line offering of man's wear. They had also been aware of Carson's reluctance to sell his name with no involvement in the manufacture and marketing of the product. Hart, Schaffner, and Marx had the necessary credentials, backed by a fine reputation, so when they approached Carson, Sonny Werblin decided to take a closer look.

Performers have always had a tremendous impact on clothing styles. In *It Happened One Night,* Gable was seen without a tee shirt; the fad caught on to such a degree that he practically ruined the industry. In the early 50s Marlon Brando repopularized the tee shirt with movies like *Streetcar Named Desire* and *The Wild One.* Retailers had reported for some time customers requesting turtlenecks and Nehru jackets "like I saw Carson wear the other night." Johnny has been called the best, or the worst dresser on television. It depends on whose idea of well dressed you adhere to, the more popular attitude being he is one of the best dressed. With a nightly show, the possibilities for promotion seemed endless.

What Hart, Schaffner and Marx had in mind was a grade 2 line of clothes with suits priced to sell in the $100 plus category and sport jackets starting around $75. It would be a high-quality ready to wear line.

After careful inspection of all the details, Johnny decided to go for it. The name of the new company would be Johnny Carson Apparel Inc. John would be the president and as such would have a great deal to say in the operation, determining where the major thrust of the new concern's marketing would be aimed, what the basic style would be, and making sure that whatever done would be carried out in the basic good taste his name had come to symbolize. Hart, Schaffner and Marx would own 51 percent of the operation, Johnny and Sonny having equal shares of the remaining stock. John would draw a salary plus profits from his stock.

Johnny Carson Apparel had made their major advertising push with magazine ads and an occasional television commercial. Direct plugs by John on the show are prohibited by the network and the FCC, but there are ways around this and John uses them all. The fact that he wears a different suit or sport jacket every night constitutes an advertisement because there are few viewers who do not know he is in the clothes business and recognize his outfits as his company's product. His constant teasing of Doc's outlandish costumes allows Doc to compliment John on his clothes; they are bright comedy bits and ring a good tune on the retailer's cash registers. Ed has always scratched John's back with mentions of his clothes, and John responds by reading the endless string of Ed's extracurricular activities.

The retailers love Johnny Carson Apparel. Not only is it a good, reasonably-priced line, but they get to use Johnny's name in advertising pitches for their stores. The entire operation has proved one of the better investments John has made. At the retail level, Johnny Carson Apparel sold $35,000,000 in 1972, making a healthy jump to $50,000,000 in 1973. No one is going to release financial details of the company, least of all John, but a reasonable rule of thumb would be a $20 profit on a $100 retail item. Heavy advertising would cut into that figure, but not enough to make John's income from Johnny Carson Apparel less than seven figures a year.

The company has now branched out into shirts, ties, belts, and jewelry, all manufactured by license.

In mid-1969, NBC gave studio 6-B a complete overhaul, redecorating at a cost of $6,000,000. To the viewing audience, it did not look that much different. Most of the money went for new production equipment to make the show easier to run. Studio 6-B has had quite a history, starting out as a radio studio for Manhattan Merry Go-Round, Basin Street, and the Bell Telephone Hour. Stars who have used the premises during their radio days include Henry Morgan, Bob Hope, and Dinah Shore. When it was converted to television use, it saw the likes of Milton Berle, Red Buttons, and Jack

Paar as well as the popular "That Was the Week That Was" and "Meet the Press."

John's association with Werblin payed big dividends in his new contract talks with NBC in July of 1969. The negotiations were handled by Robert Schulman of Wenschel, Schulman, and Manning, tax experts.

NBC president Don Durgin said Johnny got, "A good increase and one that he richly deserves." He also said the reported high of $40,000 a week was, "Ridiculous!" He refused further comment on the amount of John's paycheck. Networks never like to talk about salaries for fear of touching off new contract demands from other stars.

No sooner had NBC announced the new contract than the *New York Times* reported Johnny was now the highest paid performer on television, receiving $75,000 a week. The article went on to say that the previous highs had been Godfrey and Gary Moore, both of CBS, whose salaries were reputed to be in the $60-65,000 a week category.

John's reaction was instantaneous, "I think it's damn unfair to me and damn unfair to performers. I want to disclaim it here once and for all." The *Times* then said a portion of the settlement included a large chunk of RCA stock. John would neither confirm or deny this allegation.

Finally, enough pressure was brought by NBC and Carson to force the *Times* to reassess John's salary to a more respectable $55,000 a week. No one denied this figure too strenuously.

The big money handed out was not out of line with the enormous sums spent by the networks to keep favored stars happy. CBS once spent $750,000 for a house for Jackie Gleason, who spent very little time in it, later leaving it to CBS to dispose of at a loss.

Johnny had tried to get better office facilities for years. Slowly but surely NBC had upgraded the "Tonight Show" offices, going so far as to tear up the floor and install a toilet for John in his office. The toilet was much appreciated by John, who claimed the old facilities were so far from his office that "I have to go to the Port Authority Bus Depot to pee." Then in September 1969, right after NBC had done a

$25,000 redecoration, the new facilities were burned in a fire. The only thing to survive out of Johnny's personal effects were his set of lucky cufflinks. On the opening of the Johnny Carson "Tonight Show" a close friend had given him St. Genesius cufflinks. St. Genesius is the patron saint of actors and talk show hosts. His then fiancè, Joanne, gave him replicas of the NBC cameras used on the show, made into cufflinks. Not wanting to offend either, he wore one of each and continues to do so to this day. They were the only things lucky enough to escape the flames.

By now the talk show craze was in full swing. There was never a time when a gab fest could not be found on some channel, especially in the big cities where the independent stations were free to pick up syndicated shows during the day. CBS had decided to go with Merv and premiered him in the middle of August. Making talk the late night staple of all the networks, ABC was still going with Joey. Soon ABC would drop Joey and try the controversial route with Dick Cavett. David Frost was busily shuttling back and forth across the Atlantic doing talk shows in England as well as here. Bill Dana was still around, plus Mike Douglas. None of them had either the appeal, ratings, or the number of stations Carson had. None of them were about to challenge him as the king of the gab fests either, but the sheer weight of talk might finally get to us and we could turn them all off. Merv Griffin put it best when talking about alternative viewing for the person who did not want talk, "He can either watch us or catch the Spanish news on channel 47."

Johnny lost one of his outlets when the armed forces network dropped the show. The official reason was the number of commercials they had to work around. The real reason was the number of anti-Nixon cracks made by the guests on the show. It was no great loss to John, who had been aware for some time that he was writing the comedy material for half the comics working in England. They would pick up the armed forces broadcasts over radio and frantically write down the monologue to use in their act. After an absence of six months, the "Tonight Show" was picked up again by the armed forces network.

JOHNNY CARSON

As Johnny's position became stronger and stronger, he seemed to relax and trust himself more with his guests. The result was an even better "Tonight Show," prompting one of the greatest ad libbers, Bob Hope, to say, "There's no script. You get out there before one of the most critical audiences in the business with one of the sharpest guys ever, and you know you're in the frying pan and you just hope you stay there."

After a spate of criticism because of his lack of topicality compared to the recent "Dick Cavett Show," most performers came around to compliment John. The new praise emboldened John to take one last shot at those who complained of the lack of "relevance," the late '60s and early '70s favorite word. "I get irked when the press says my show doesn't do enough relevant things. Neither does Dean Martin or Flip Wilson. That's up to Bill Buckley. The idea of television, as I understand it, is to reach as many people as possible. That's one measure of success." And by that yardstick John measured up, and knew it. "Or you can do prison reform and other 'relevant' things. If you do that, you're not going to reach the people. David Frost did that and for some reason he doesn't seem to be on anymore."

Johnny is right if you are trying to reach the numbers he does, but there should be room for prison reform on late-night television also. The answer lies in the other networks realization that they will have to be happy with a smaller share of the audience when they go opposite Carson, and not cancel excellent shows because they are unable to take John's audience away.

With his new sense of security and longer vacations, John has let bigger stars sit behind the desk in his absence. When John returned they would inevitably drop by soon after as a guest, shaking their heads in amazement, "I don't know how you do it, John." John would smile and the audience would applaud, "This has got to be the toughest damn job in all of teleivision." John would smile again and say thank you and quickly move on to another subject. He already knew how rough the job is. Star after star paraded onto the show with compliments for the same work they had criticized him for

186

years before. Johnny was polite enough not to say "I told you so."

In the show business community a familiar refrain goes something like this, "Yeah? What are you in now?" Working, mere survival is an accomplishment to be applauded, but constant employment on the biggest hot seat in television was finally realized for what it was and accordingly lauded.

Whether Johnny no longer needed the security of walling himself up inside his marriage, thirty-nine floors above the street, or he wanted out for other reasons, he left Joanne after six years of an inseparable marriage.

Johnny reportedly had urged Joanne to get out of the house and involve herself with activities other than the occasional charity and her regular appearances on a local astrology television show "Guess My Sign." These seemed strange requests coming from a man of Johnny's reputation. After telling her on several occasions that he wanted a divorce, he locked her out of the apartment in the early spring of 1969. with nowhere to go, Joanne went to live with the Henry Fondas, Shirlee Fonda being one of her closest friends. John called several times and went over to the house. Joanne claims he wanted to keep a relationship with her, but no longer wanted to be married. She also voiced her desire to remain married to John, pleading total innocence in provoking him to take the action he did.

She filed a divorce separation suit charging John with cruel and inhuman treatment, abandonment, and adultery. Her lawyers asked for $7,000 a week in alimony. John's lawyers announced shortly thereafter they had reached an "amicable agreement" and Joanne's lawyers withdrew the demand for $7,000 a week.

In the middle of all this, which goes to prove that John was not that much different from thousands of other American parents of this era, his son Ricky was busted for possession of marijuana in Cranston, Rhode Island. He was released on a $1000 personal recognizance bond.

Renowned as being tight with his coins, John was honestly staggered by Joanne's alimony demands and got many miles out of it on the show. Joanne put a stop to that in January of

1972 by sueing John for breaching an agreement not to
slander or slur each other in public. She asked $125,000.
John stopped doing alimony jokes.

In June of 1972, after much legal maneuvering on both
sides, Joanne got a final divorce decree. In court she sobbed
her story to the judge, telling him how John had locked her
out of their apartment. "He was abusive to me and I feared
for my mental and physical health," she wept.

"Try to compose youself," counseled the judge, "It is not
unique. Thousands wind up here."

The decree was granted and in her statement to the press
she said "He was my first and only love. I'm still in love with
the guy." She had her wedding band melted down and recast
into a teardrop. It is now silver plated and hangs around her
neck constantly. "Johnny is a genius. I'm still his number one
fan, but I wasn't cut out to be married to such a high
achiever. For ten years I was living on the ragged edge of his
genius."

It had always been a part of every one of John's contracts
with NBC that he would not have to do the show from the
West Coast. Joanne, in an effort to get away from everything
connected with Johnny, had moved to the West Coast.
Whether it was coincidental or not is a moot point, but
shortly thereafter John made it known that he would now
like to have the show based in Los Angeles. Joanne says he
followed because, "I think he just wanted to be near me."

Once in Los Angeles, Joanne landed her own television
show. The kitchen set of the show was an exact replica of
their old kitchen in the couple's former apartment. The show
featured guest celebrities whose agents would call the
"Tonight Show" offices for permission to appear on Joanne's
show. When they asked if their clients would be jeopardizing
their chances with the "Tonight Show" by appearing with
Joanne, the answer they usually got was best described as
"noncommittal."

As with his previous wife, Johnny demanded and got an
agreement never to reveal details of their life together. Precise
information from the thirty-two page separation agreement is
impossible to obtain. Estimates of the alimony that so upset

John range from $200,000 cash plus $200,000 in art and $100,000 a year in alimony, all the way up to $2,000,000 in cash in addition to undisclosed property plus all the rest.

According to John, his reason for moving the "Tonight Show" to Los Angeles had nothing to do with Joanne. John claims he moved because practically all nighttime television programming originated in Los Angeles. That was where the stars were. Television stars, yes, but motion picture and stage personalities remain spread all over. "The craftsmen and technical people have left. It's tough to do a show in New York," was the next reason given. But that one held no more water than the one before it.

When asked if he could find good young performers as he had in New York Johnny said, "It's nice to say you're going to go to these terrific little clubs and discover new talent, but where in the hell are they? Night life in New York City, when you come right down to it, hasn't been good for years." True, all the club acts were now either in Las Vegas, Miami, or foreign resorts, not in New York . . . or Los Angeles.

Finally peeved with the demands for a rational answer, John told the truth of the matter: it doesn't matter where the "Tonight Show" comes from. "The 'Tonight Show' isn't in New York or Hollywood. It's at the end of the bed. Right where I want it to be," John explained.

NBC built a one and a half million dollar annex to their Burbank studios to accommodate the "Tonight Show" staff, and just recently spent many more dollars on a complete new set. Every guest on the night of its unveiling commented on its tackiness.

After getting to California, John was forced to take two weeks off from the show because of an attack of hepatitis. One of the benefits of California, Rona Barret, the syndicated gossip, said "Not so! Johnny Carson took two weeks off to have cosmetic surgery performed on his face to remove bags under his eyes." Take your pick.

After it was revealed that the lead used in making tubes for toothpaste might pose a health hazard, Johnny mentioned it in his monologue. NBC cut the remark out of the monologue at the request of Crest toothpaste, one of the "Tonight

Show" sponsors. This time Johnny called in the FCC, maintaining his freedom of speech had been violated.

In California Johnny was seen much more socially than he ever was in New York. He had now become a tennis buff and had many of his tennis pals on the show.

Any person in the public light as much as John draws a lunatic fringe—people who write threatening letters. While in New York, the "Tonight Show" mail was filled by a voodoo freak who kept sending bits of toilet paper soaked in blood. There is practically no way of avoiding this type of thing. John would turn them all over to the police and nothing would ever come of it. In October of 1972, someone who was more serious threatened Johnny. It was an extortion plot, and just to prove he meant business, the extortionist placed a grenade on Johnny's front steps. The demand was for $250,000. John, once again, turned over all information to the police, who instructed him to go along with the demands. The police would stake out the proposed payoff location and protect John in the process. Here the story takes a bizarre turn.

On the appointed night John drove to the proscribed telephone booth to make contact with the extortionist. After receiving instructions, John got back into his car and drove to the designated location. The phone booth where he had made the call was located outside a Launderette. There a young man, Richard Culkin, and his wife saw Johnny in the booth, and like true Johnny Carson fans raced out of the launderette to say hello to the star. By this time John had gotten back into his car and was driving to his rendezvous. Culkin immediately raced to his car and followed John to the drop-off point. The police had observed all this and shadowed both cars. As Carson neared the drop-off point, the police swooped down, nabbing one Richard Dziabacinski in addition to Culkin and his wife, who they ordered out of their car at shotgun point.

Culkin related his side of the story, but the police refused to believe him, choosing to try and beat the information out of him. After hitting him over thirty times, Culkin gave them no new information. Next they put Culkin in one of the police cars and took him out onto the freeway where they opened the back door and held Culkin's head out in a last effort to make him talk. Culkin had nothing to say, except, "I'd like to talk to a lawyer."

Four months later, Dziabacinski confessed to placing what turned out to be a dummy grenade on John's front steps.

The "Tonight Show" was going better than ever, his night-club career was in full swing, and John was finally getting the acclaim he always felt he deserved. When he was on the show, he pushed his chair back from the desk and allowed himself to genuinely laugh at other artist's material much more often. After two marriages, four television shows of his own, and countless hassles with the business end of the medium, itwas becoming apparent that Johnny Carson was indeed much happier than he had been making $47 a week in Omaha.

On the tenth anniversary of John's start on the "Tonight Show," they threw a celebration. Dave Tebit of the "Tonight Show" staff organized the entire thing. It was held in the Crystal Room of the Beverly Hills Hotel. It was an all-star affair, with hardly anyone of any consequence in the West Coast entertainment world absent. The affair started routinely enough for Hollywood with the presentation of a cake over twice Johnny's height. John stepped up to the huge piece of confectionary and said, "A lot of columnists have been asking why me and my gal haven't set a date for the wedding." He was referring to his constant companion Joanna Holland, a beautiful 26-year-old model. "So I think I will tell you that we were married at 1:30 this afternoon."

If the show is John's, the surprises are John's. He took her hand and in a rare display of public emotion said, "I love her very much, so we were married this afternoon in southern California. I thank you all for coming."

The notice in *Variety* tersely stated: "Joanna Holland to Johnny Carson. Sept. 30th, Santa Monica, Calif. Bride is a model. Groom host of NBC-TV's 'Tonight Show.' Her first. His third."

As the celebration got into full swing, Johnny found that he was not the only one with a surprise. He was ready for the toasts and tributes, he had heard most of them before, but the warmth and sincerity of the guests in praising him went beyond anything he had ever expected.

Don Rickles conducted the entertainment with his usual insults mixed with more than his usual compliments. Later in the night when Don really got rolling in his own fashion, Johnny cooled him down with, "I've been on for ten years. You've been on for ten weeks. You've already killed two networks, don't kill mine. From now on it's armed forces radio for you."

One at a time, they paid tribute to a man who had been instrumental in so many of their careers. Flip Wilson, who got his start on the "Tonight Show," Rowan and Martin, Goerge Burns (who did not get his start on the "Tonight Show"), Bob Newhart, Carl Reiner, Jack Benny, the list went on forever. Rosalind Russell put it best in her toast to the new couple, "I'd like to wish you half the joy you've given others." She was followed by Joey Bishop, and Don Adams, and Red Foxx, whose tribute turned the air so blue it was difficult to see the next person. Johnny loved it, practically falling to the floor laughing.

At the end, Johnny stood, choked with emotion, "I hope I never get too sophisticated and too inured to say I don't appreciate all this. I never thought I'd reach the point in my life when I would have this measure of success and to have these people say all these things, it's really what it's all about and I thank you." There is no question that he meant that from the deepest part of his soul.

It was a night John will always remember. Tebit had done everything humanly possible to make it the biggest night in John's life, running here and there to make sure that everything went just right. Someone mentioned Tebit went about the preparations as if it were Johnny's Bar Mitzvah. It was a good party. The total cost came to a little bit less than one minute of commercial time on the show.

After Johnny stopped demanding the accolades, they finally came. It is agreed with almost total consensus that what John does is unique, good, and what the American public wants, and the best part about it all is that it is what John wants too.

JOHNNY CARSON

"I think you can tell I'm having fun out there. I love the applause, the cheers, and sometimes when an audience rises to their feet . . . that's a hell of a thrill! It's great to go home in the evening and know you've entertained thousands of people. I wanted to be an entertainer and to be myself and I've made it."